Geikie Gorge National Park, Western Australia

National Parks of Western Australia & the Northern Territory

National Parks of Western Australia & The Northern Territory

READER'S DIGEST

The editors wish to thank the officers of the Department of
Conservation and Land Management of Western Australia, the Conservation Commission of the Northern
Territory and the Australian National Parks and Wildlife Service for their advice
and assistance; in particular, Cliff Winfield, Kevin Goss, Sweton Stewart, Shona Whitfield and Chris Mobbs.

Some of the material in this book first appeared in
Reader's Digest Wild Australia, first published in 1984;
republished in 1998.

**WILD AUSTRALIA was edited and designed by
Reader's Digest (Australia) Pty Limited**

All travelling photographic commissions were
undertaken by Robin Morrison

Project Editor	Art Editor
David Underhill	Anita Sattler

Editor • Robert Campbell
Assistant Editor • Françoise Toman
Research Editor • Vere Dodds

READER'S DIGEST NATIONAL PARKS OF WESTERN AUSTRALIA AND THE NORTHERN TERRITORY was edited and designed by
Reader's Digest (Australia) Pty Limited

Project Editor	**Art Editor**
Shirley Macnab	Anita Sattler

FIRST EDITION 1987, SECOND EDITION 1998
Published by Reader's Digest (Australia) Pty Limited
26 - 32 Waterloo Street, Surry Hills, NSW 2010.

Copyright © Reader's Digest (Australia) Pty Limited 1987, 1998
Copyright © Reader's Digest (New Zealand) Limited 1987, 1998
Copyright © Reader's Digest Association Far East Limited 1987, 1998
Philippines Copyright © Reader's Digest Association Far East Limited 1987, 1998

All rights reserved. No part of this book may be reproduced, stored in a retrieval
system, or transmitted in any form or by any means, electronic, electrostatic,
magnetic tape, mechanical, photocopying, recording or otherwise, without
permission in writing from the publishers.

® Reader's Digest, The Digest and the Pegasus logo are registered
trademarks of The Reader's Digest Association, Inc., of Pleasantville, New York, USA.

National Library of Australia Cataloguing-in-Publication data:
National parks of Western Australia and the Northern Territory.

Includes index.
ISBN 0 86449 334 7.

1. National parks and reserves – Western Australia –
Guide-books. 2. National parks and reserves – Northern
Territory – Guide-books. 3. Western Australia –
Description and travel – 1976- – Guide-books.
4. Northern Territory – Description and travel –
1976- – Guide-books. I. Reader's Digest Services.

919.41'04

Contents

Introduction 7

PART ONE:
The nature of Australia 8

How the stage was set 10

Sun and rain: the great dictators 12

Grandeur in the high country 14

Fresh water: a precious bounty 16

Where the oceans hold sway 18

The eternal battle of the trees 20

Rainforests: a squandered heritage 22

The forests that welcome fire 24

Sentinels of the never-never 26

PART TWO:
Parks and people 28

Why we have national parks 30

Jacks and Jills of all trades 32

Staying alive in the bush 34

How the public can help 36

Making the most of your visit 37

WILDLIFE: Where animals find safety 38

RESTORATION: Nature gets another chance 40

HERITAGE: An obligation to the world 42

PART THREE:
A guide to the national parks of Western Australia and the Northern Territory 44

ESPERANCE & ALBANY REGIONS 46

Directory of parks 68

PERTH REGION 70

Directory of parks 91

Mammals and reptiles of Western Australia 94

CARNARVON & PORT HEDLAND REGIONS 96

Directory of parks 105

DERBY & KUNUNURRA REGIONS 106

Directory of parks 115

Flowers as food 116

VISITOR ACTIVITIES 118

DARWIN REGION 120

Directory of parks 137

Wildlife in the Territory 138

ALICE SPRINGS REGION 140

Directory of parks 161

Reptiles of the inland 162

VISITOR ACTIVITIES 164

Index 166

Acknowledgments 168

Kakadu National Park, Northern Territory

INTRODUCTION
What's in a name?

AUSTRALIA HAS more than 500 so-called national parks. Their status was proclaimed by state and territorial authorities under policies that used to differ widely. Many parks, especially among the 300-odd declared in Queensland, are mere islets or scraps of bush as small as one hectare. Some are huge, but so remote and inhospitable that their existence has little public relevance. And in a few parks, visitors have no place at all – the sites are really animal sanctuaries, or strictly for research.

Nature reserves of that sort are important. But people expect direct benefits from something called a national park. The term should denote a significant area capable of accommodating the right of substantial numbers of visitors to enjoy its natural features and learn from them. Too many 'parks' do not meet this prescription. Bestowed indiscriminately, a proud title loses meaning. The effect, though surely not intended, is sometimes to mislead and disappoint the public.

In offering a frank comparison of park attractions, we aim not to dictate readers' tastes but to provide them with a fair basis for making choices of their own. This guide presents a revision of information first amassed in the Reader's Digest book *Wild Australia*. That remains the only single publication to appraise such a large number of the country's national parks.

Simply identifying all of them for the first edition demanded a trailblazing effort. Because of the pace of acquisition and change since the 1950s, no complete list had existed. Even the names of some parks were difficult to establish. Legally gazetted titles conflicted with common usage, or hard-pressed administrators saved paperwork by lumping smaller sites anonymously into groups.

Financial strictures beset all parks services. Areas may be designated by the stroke of a pen, but funds for public facilities are a long time coming. Often as our researchers sought to define the merits of a park, they were told: 'We'd really rather you didn't mention that one'. A state information officer, confessing his ignorance of a newly acquired property, explained: 'We sent a fellow out there once to get material for a brochure. But he couldn't find the place...'

Not without qualms, a system of rating was instituted. Judgments behind all the ticks and crosses in the reference sections were made in consultation with park authorities, but they remain subjective and debatable. So are our assumptions of the broad areas of visitor interest. 'Scenic enjoyment' in one park derives from the intimate charm of a single waterfall; in another it may come from the sweeping grandeur of a whole mountain range or coastline. 'Day activities' indicates a good choice of things to do – but who can predict preferences? 'Family camping' supposes a desire to stay put for perhaps a week, in conditions not unduly primitive. 'Hard bushwalking' in most cases points to the challenge of backpack trekking and overnight camping.

Pictorially we have aimed for realism, not idealism. Rather than gathering in a selection of the prettiest and luckiest shots ever taken in national parks, we offer the results of one man's efforts. Robin Morrison, the touring photographer, was advised and guided by rangers in some parks. But for the most part he took his chances like any other member of the travelling public, limited in time and at the mercy of the weather.

After his year-long assignment for *Wild Australia*, covering more than 200 locations from Tasmania to North West Cape, Morrison had a suggestion. 'Tell your readers,' he said, 'that anything I did, they can do. With any luck they may see even more. And you can also tell them that most of the finest scenery in this country is not all that far away or hard to get to.'

He was right. In spite of the obvious modification of desirable countryside by two centuries of European settlement, unspoilt landscapes lie remarkably close to most major centres of population. Australians, nearly 90 per cent of whom lead their everyday lives in urban or suburban environments, need not go far to refresh themselves and recover their sense of community with more natural surroundings.

This book is published in the hope that readers will reach a fuller understanding of what remains of our physical heritage, that they will care for it, and above all that they will enjoy it.

THE EDITORS

PART ONE
The nature of Australia

Nothing in nature happens without a reason. Powerful influences shaped Australia's landscapes. Now they dictate where its unique plants grow. Knowing the meaning that lies behind scenery makes it all the more enjoyable.

Ancient but scarcely trodden, the Bungle Bungle Ranges stand in lonely dignity east of the Kimberleys, WA

THE NATURE OF AUSTRALIA

How the stage was set

WEATHERING, given time enough, levels any land surface. Heights are worn down and basins are filled with the debris, to be compressed into fresh rock. With the ups and downs removed and gravity equalised, rock erosion stops. Only overlying soils or sands are subject to further attack.

But awesome pressures work tirelessly on the earth's crust. Sometimes they warp it, tilting an old land mass to a new angle of elevation. Sometimes the crust buckles, and another generation of mountains is thrust up. Molten material from below blasts or oozes through weak points in the crust. The height of the land is varied and erosion resumes. All these events have occurred time and again in Australia.

Rocks of the Australian land mass differ astonishingly in their age, their composition and their capacity to resist erosion. They include the world's oldest known formations as well as some of the youngest, and everything from the softest clays to the most impermeable granites. Climatic conditions vary widely. So do the surrounding oceans in their behaviour – some destroy the land, some help it to build. Most diverse of all are the soils produced by rock erosion, and the plant life they can sustain.

Flat landscapes, virtually featureless and usually parched, prevail across more than half of the continent. Weathering is all but complete, for much of this land has been undisturbed for eons. Ranges thrust up in the west, made from rocks that formed more than 3000 million years ago, are reduced to a smoothed shield, rarely outcropping from its sandy cover. Once-mighty rivers that drained the heights – and helped demolish them – can be traced only in chains of dismal salt pans. Seabeds to the east have become plains, at best marginally fertile.

Remnants of mountain systems in Central Australia and the far north and northwest are younger, though the age of their rocks still staggers the mind. Ranges such as the Musgraves and the Hamersleys, along with many in the Kimberleys and Arnhem Land, originated more than 1000 million years ago. Pushed up, they towered higher than Mt Kosciusko is now. All are in the late stages of destruction – but nature has not wasted them.

By the time the MacDonnell Ranges were forced up in Central Australia, perhaps 200-300 million years ago, material eroded from the Musgraves had re-formed as a bed of sedimentary rock. South of the MacDonnells, it was distorted and broken by their upheaval. Immense chunks of sandstone or cemented boulders were elevated at all angles, to be swamped later by a returning sea. New deposits of sediments buried all but the highest summits. Now, severely worn in their turn, the broad domes we call Ayers Rock and the Olgas jut incongruously from the central plain.

Nearby Mt Conner, similarly created, presents a surprising contrast. It is table-topped, and noticeably eroded only at the sides. When this mass was pushed up, its layers of sediments chanced to remain horizontal under their original capping of toughened material. To the north, on apparently similar country, are piled the huge boulders called the Devil's Marbles. Here a cracked block of granite has been eroded across and down all its joints. Such variations are essentially the products of chance – what types of rocks are exposed, and how their former bedding planes are tilted.

Ocean levels rose and fell – or the land fell and rose – repeatedly. Invading seas often divided ancestral Australia into islands. New rock material included increasing quantities of calcium from the remains of marine animals. Pavings of porous limestone formed widely. High and dry now, many are noted for their subterranean cave systems, eaten out by percolating rainwater.

Sometimes the seas were remarkably warm. Corals built reefs in the Gordon River district of Tasmania 350-400 million years ago. But 100 million years later an icecap reached to the Kimberleys, and Tasmania lay beside the South Pole. And after a further 100 million years, according to plant fossil evidence, Australia and Antarctica shared a subtropical climate. Like all continental land masses, they have been on the move.

At first all the continents were probably contained in a single cluster, which seems to have broken in two well over 200 million years ago. After that Australia, Antarctica, New Guinea, India, Africa, Arabia and South America were joined in a southern supercontinent which scientists call Gondwanaland. But the earth's rigid crust was fracturing. Rifts opened, and new molten matter welled up to force the modern continents apart.

Widening oceans filled the gaps. The crust

Eroded rock layers at Kings Canyon, NT, are tilted almost vertically. Once they formed towering domes

TRACING A VANISHED LANDSCAPE

ROCKS are of three types. Sedimentary rocks form from the debris of older rocks and the remains of aquatic animals. Sandstones, limestones and shales are commonest. Igneous rocks form from molten material. If it cools without reaching the air, it usually turns into granite. Lava cooling on the surface makes a basalt. Metamorphic rocks are the result of pressure and heat on sedimentary or igneous rocks. Sandstone becomes quartzite, shale becomes slate, granite becomes gneiss.

Sedimentary rocks form in flat layers, varying in hardness. Squeezed by earth movements, they bend into folds. Erosion removes the softer material in a fold, and only the stubs of tough ridges remain

Molten material pushing up into a fold forms granite. Erosion leaves a tough core (left). But if the material builds a volcano, the last of it may set as a hard-wearing plug of trachyte or rhyolite (right)

Beds of metamorphic rock are too rigid to fold. Instead they crack into blocks that are tilted and pushed up. Rates of erosion depend on the angle of tilt, as well as on the composition of the blocks

The west's ancient granite shield snapped near Perth

itself separated into mobile plates. Fifteen major plates and a few small ones now restlessly cover the globe. The section Australia rides on – along with India, New Guinea and part of New Zealand – is rafting very slowly northwestward because its eastern and southern neighbours are expanding.

Violent earth movements are inevitable at the edges of a plate. But Australia lies far from any collision zone. Since its isolation it has been the least disturbed of the continents. The last truly catastrophic event – the production of eastern and central Tasmania's dolerite columns and cappings by the intrusion of molten matter into old sandstones – was about 165 million years ago. Many geologists associate it with the start of the Gondwanaland breakup.

Early mountain ranges on the eastern mainland were well worn down by then. Soon all that remained of them were cores of tough granite, solidified from molten material that had flowed up into their folds. Often it is this granite that forms the summits of mountains that have been thrust up more recently.

Parts of the Eastern Highlands – notably the Snowy Mountains and Victorian Alps – were pushed up about 65 million years ago. A second phase of general uplift in the east, remarkably gentle, took place within the past 3-7 million years. A probable cause was the slumping of the crust far inland, under the weight of sediments from one ocean or sea after another. The slumped parts, since covered by more recent porous rock, underlie the reservoirs of underground water known collectively as the Great Artesian Basin.

To compensate for this sinking of the crust, land near the east coast gradually rose. It formed tablelands with a barely perceptible slope. Warping to create mountain ranges occurred only in the last stages of uplift, and at the seaward extremity. Similar forces working in the west had a more drastic effect. There the ancient rock shield was pinned down by coastal sediments. It snapped at the point where it emerged, and now its uptilted edge forms a rampart nearly 1000 km long backing the coastal plain on which Perth is centred. The Darling Range is misnamed – it should be the Darling Scarp. But in its influence on climate and vegetation, it acts in much the same way as a mountain system would.

Near-coastal ranges and the coastlines themselves have the freshest and most changeable landforms. All the forces of erosion are seen actively at work. Volcanic activity can be traced. So can the variation of soil fertilities, and the rivalries of plant communities under different climatic regimes. Everywhere, the lie of the land and the look of the landscape are intimately related.

THE OLDEST THING ON EARTH

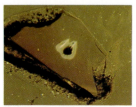

Electric probing mars a history-making zircon – enlarged 200 times

OUR PLANET was born 4500-4600 million years ago, astronomers believe. It took an unknown time to cool enough to form a solid crust. The most ancient rocks found, in Western Australia and Greenland, are about 3800 million years old. But they are sedimentary – made of something even older.

A clue emerged in 1983 at Mt Narryer, 200 km inland from Carnarvon, WA. Microscopic grains of zircon were discovered in quartzite rocks. Using a new electrical probing technique, scientists measured the proportions of uranium and lead contained as impurities in the zircons.

Uranium loses its radioactivity and turns into lead at a known rate. So the age of the zircons could be calculated. Four of the tiny stones, it seems, must have been formed between 4100 and 4200 million years ago. Until humans venture outside this solar system, they may never handle anything older.

THE NATURE OF AUSTRALIA

Sun and rain: the great dictators

JUST AS ancient weathering shaped the land, present climates decide its clothing. Sunlight, temperature and moisture determine which trees or shrubs or grasses flourish where. And they govern the likelihood of wildfire – the other factor that sets apart the great plant families of Australia and rules over the appearance of natural landscapes.

Twisting statistics, Australians could boast the world's most generous share of rain. More of it falls, per person, than in any other country. But that is merely a reflection of the sparseness of population. In fact most of the continent is poorly watered and subject to high rates of evaporation. Over a vast sweep between southwestern Queensland and North West Cape, hot sunshine beats down for more than 3500 hours a year.

Mainland Australia straddles the southern hemisphere's belt of greatest air pressure. 'Highs' – cells of descending air as much as 4000 km wide, calm or rotating gently under clear skies – pass from west to east in an almost continuous chain. Troughs separating them, usually at intervals of four or five days, may bring cool changes but seldom much rain. North of the pressurised belt southeasterly breezes – the Trade Winds of sailing ship days – blow steadily from the Pacific. To the south of the belt the air flow is from the west, and much stronger.

The high-pressure belt changes its position seasonally. In winter it is centred over the middle of the continent. Tropical regions, except on the east coast, are parched. The southeasterlies, having deposited their ocean moisture on the coastal ranges, flow on unimpeded and arrive in the northwest dry, hot and dusty.

Southern Australia in winter is swept by a cold westerly air stream. Often this is whipped into chilling southwesterly gales because 'lows' – tight, churning cells of rising and condensing air – intrude from the Southern Ocean. Rain is plentiful, except round the Bight, and the southeastern highlands get snow. But in much of New South Wales and subtropical Queensland, where the westerlies have dried out or do not reach, winter may be sunny.

In summer the belt of high pressure lies over Bass Strait. Rainfall is generally low in southern regions, though clear spells may be broken by squally changes. On most parts of the east coast down to Sydney, however, Pacific moisture is turned into liberal summer rains because the Trade Winds have also moved south.

From November to April, the far north has its 'Wet'. A zone of low pressure, originating over the Equator but shifting in summer to about the latitude of Darwin, sucks in a monsoon of saturated air from the northwest. Thundery showers drench the Kimberleys, the Top End and Cape York Peninsula day after day. In some seasons, but never predictably, the lows pass far enough south to bring flooding rains to Central Australia and outback regions of the southern and eastern states.

Summer is also the season of violent tropical cyclones. Only five or six a year affect the coast, and their destructive power wanes as soon as they pass inland. But the spiralling cloud mass of a decaying cyclone brings heavy rain over an ever-widening area, perhaps for a week or more. Semi-arid regions, particularly in the northwest, receive much of their moisture in this erratic way.

Regardless of average patterns, year-by-year rainfall over most of Australia is notoriously variable. Port Hedland, WA, for example, is listed as having a median annual fall of just over 300 mm. But that figure is merely the product of actual readings as low as 30 mm a year and as high as 1000 mm or more. Apart from the monsoon zone, rainfall is consistently good only in Tasmania, on most of the Victorian, New South Wales and Queensland coasts, and in winter in the extreme southwest of Western Australia. It is no coincidence that all these regions have mountains close to the sea.

Air flowing off sunlit oceans is always loaded with evaporated moisture. But to condense into clouds that precipitate rain, it must be cooled. The usual cause of cooling is elevation: air temperatures drop by about 5°C with each 1000 metres of altitude. A fall in pressure when air flows into a 'low', or a collision of different air masses, can cause the necessary uplift and trigger a storm. However, no one can say exactly where that will happen. Truly reliable rains occur only where moist air flows are blocked and forced upward by steep land.

Australia is not only the flattest of all continents, but also the lowest-lying. Counting mountain ranges, its average elevation is still a mere 300 metres above sea level. That makes it generally warmer than any other land mass in comparable latitudes. Far from being cooled, moist air flowing into many regions is heated up. The longer its journey, the hotter it gets – hence the heat waves that occasionally sear southern cities, including Hobart.

Summer northwesterlies, entering over the Great Sandy Desert between Port Hedland and Broome, have the longest possible low, flat run. If not diverted by atmospheric disturbances they can reach all the way to western NSW – 2500 km. Shade temperatures above 50°C are recorded there, in an arc from Bourke to Wilcannia and White Cliffs, more often than in any other district in Australia.

Superheated air flows hasten the evaporation of soil moisture and the desiccation of plants. In regions perennially short of rain – though with fertile soil – plant life has had to adapt in unusual ways. And where rains in most years are good enough to foster profuse growth, but they occasionally fail, the chance of devastation by fire is abnormally high. Again plants have found ways to cope – and even to benefit.

At the opposite end of the climatic scale, wide tracts of high country in the southeast and Tasmania lie under snow for months each year. Elsewhere, over a surprising area, plants contend with frost in winter and spring. In the south it results from inflows of chilled air after depressions. But frosts also occur well to the north, in places better known for their heat. In the high-pressure belt dominating mid-Australia in winter, cloud cover is rare and ground warmth starts passing into the upper atmosphere as soon as the sun goes down. Alice Springs has more frosty nights than any of the southern capitals except Canberra. On the east coast, the effects of elevation take frosts even farther north. Cooled air, sinking into valleys draining the Great Dividing Range, can ice the ground within 20 km of Cairns.

Parched, sunburnt sandplains reach into NSW at Mungo National Park – once part of a major waterway

Below: Air cooling over Kosicuszko National Park, NSW, sinks into the upper Murray Valley, forming a river of cloud

Right: Highland frost and vigorous tree growth join forces to crack capping rock in Girraween National Park, Qld

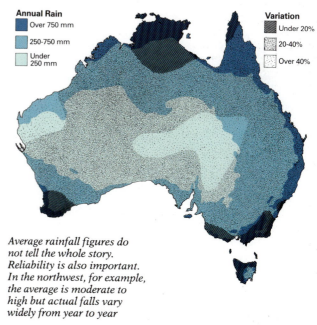

Average rainfall figures do not tell the whole story. Reliability is also important. In the northwest, for example, the average is moderate to high but actual falls vary widely from year to year

THE NATURE OF AUSTRALIA
Grandeur in the high country

MOUNTAINS are nature's showcases. Bared, they display every type and formation of rock. Erosion can be seen in action, with the effects of rain, wind, frost and chemical change accentuated by the force of gravity. And on vegetated slopes, the temperature gradients created by altitude give plant and animal life their fullest opportunity for variety.

Australia lacks the soaring peaks of the other continents and even of its island neighbours, New Guinea and New Zealand. In compensation, its high country is more accessible and less subject to dangerously sudden switches of weather. Its coastal uplands, especially in Queensland, offer a range of plant communities as wide as any in the world.

Scenically and economically, the Eastern Highlands chain is Australia's most significant mountain system. It curves from Cape York into western Victoria, more or less parallel to the coast, and resumes in Tasmania. Islands in Bass and Torres Straits, along with some off Queensland, are peaks emerging from drowned sections of the same system.

For most of their mainland length the highlands are the more elevated seaward side of a wide belt of tablelands. The Great Divide – where rivers start to flow inland, not to the Pacific Ocean – often occurs at lower altitudes well to the west. That shows how slowly the highlands rose in their final uplift, which was completed about 3 million years ago. Ancient rivers, already flowing east, had time to cut deeper courses as the land tipped up.

Movement was so gentle that buckling to produce ranges of fold mountains was limited to the eastern edge of the belt. Massive tilting of fractured blocks, to raise processions of peaks like the Southern Alps of New Zealand, was virtually non-existent. A spectacular exception is the Bellenden Ker Range, just south of Cairns, Qld. Even the summits of the Snowy Mountains and Victorian Alps are smooth granite tablelands. The Blue Mountains, west of Sydney, were just as flat. Layers of sandstone and shale were pushed up thousands of metres without shifting from their horizontal plane. Today's dramatic pillars, cliffs and ravines are simply the result of weathering – and it is far from finished.

Remnants of huge volcanic systems abound, especially about the Qld/NSW border and to the southwest in the Nandewar and Warrumbungle Ranges. These date from 15-25 million years ago. The later phase of eastern uplift brought new activity, but no big volcanoes were built. Most eruptions were easy upwellings of lava from fissures in the earth's crust.

Left: Glaciers sculpted the jagged peaks and walled lakes of southwest Tasmania

Most of the Great Dividing Range is a tableland cut by rivers – in this case the Shoalhaven River in Morton National Park, NSW

Worn quartzite domes in the Gammon Ranges, SA

Hard basalt from ancient lava flows caps Mt Wilson, 950 metres up in Blue Mountains National Park, NSW

Lava flows continued, in fewer and fewer places, almost to the present day. The last coatings on the western plains of Victoria, where more than 20 000 square kilometres are covered, were laid less than 6000 years ago. Even more of the northern Queensland tablelands was blanketed not long before.

Old volcanoes are often marked now by cylinders of rock jutting into the sky. These are plugs made of the last molten material, solidified before it reached the air. It forms exceptionally hard rock – usually trachyte or rhyolite – that resists erosion while the surrounding cone is worn away.

Molten material that flows out as lava, however, turns into a basalt. Its hardness will vary according to its mineral content. Some basalts, reddish or chocolate brown and rich in iron, remain as protective cappings on tablelands or form thin bands sandwiched in the joints of older rocks. Others, cooling evenly in deep layers, have contracted into clusters of tough hexagonal columns – Melbourne's Organ Pipes, for example.

But many basalts decompose quickly when exposed to air and water. They break down into fine, dark soils containing an unusual abundance of mineral nutrients for plants. It is the prevalence of basaltic – often called volcanic – soils, allied with high rainfall, that allows the Eastern Highlands their luxuriant growth of forests.

Tasmania's heights reveal a much older geological background. The region's main upheaval came 165 million years ago. Enormous tongues of molten material penetrated its original sandstone strata. They cooled as dolerite, which has a columnar 'organ pipe' structure similar to some basalts. Now, with almost all of the sandstone worn away, deep sheets of dolerite cover most of eastern and central Tasmania. Sheer-faced crags jut from a tableland so toughly capped that no rivers of significance have managed to cut courses. Instead this is a landscape sculpted by ice. Only in Tasmania can the full effects of glaciation during the last ice age, between 40 000 and 10 000 years ago, be seen. Mountains are chewed away at their sides. Moraines of rock debris trap deep alpine lakes. Countless little tarns, gouged by boulders dragged in a creeping cap of ice, glitter on the plateau.

West of the tableland, Tasmania's ranges have no intrusion of dolerite. They are of softer quartzite, now deeply dissected by gorges. High volumes of water, precipitated almost year-round in rain and snow, seize their chance to find steep courses to the sea between thickly forested slopes. Here are born the island's fast-flowing 'wild rivers', so enticing and precious to white-water adventurers.

No other mountains in Australia stand as tall as the Eastern Highlands, or have soils and rainfall to sustain comparable forest growth. Elsewhere the greatest fascination of higher country usually lies in its stark antiquity. The huge island-mountains of Uluru National Park, for example, or the eroded forms of the Flinders Ranges in South Australia, are individually more haunting than any eastern scene.

Major ranges in Central Australia and the northwest, such as the MacDonnells, the Hamersleys and those in the Kimberleys, are so aged and weathered that their heights lend them little distinction. Instead it is their depths, in the gorges cut by eons-old rivers, which provide the most memorable scenes – and the clearest insights into the structure of the continent.

THIS WAS THE HOTTEST SPOT OF ALL

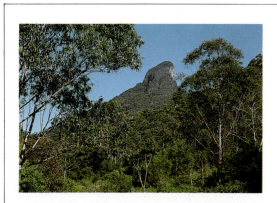

MOUNT WARNING (left) is the 22-million-year-old central plug of Australia's biggest volcano. Remnants of its rim, straddling the Qld/NSW border across a diameter of about 40 km, survive in the McPherson, Tweed and Nightcap Ranges. All have steep scarps of tough basalt facing in towards Mt Warning, and gently sloping outer flanks.

Scientists can only guess at the original dimensions of the Tweed volcano, but it almost certainly stood taller than Mt Kosciusko is now. Rainforests ringing the rim, largely preserved in a chain of national parks, flourish on rich soils derived from the volcano's outpourings of lava. It is thought to have been active for about 3 million years.

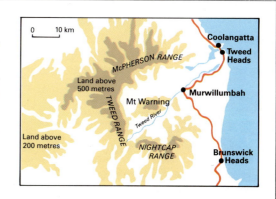

THE NATURE OF AUSTRALIA

Fresh water: a precious bounty

RIVERS AND LAKES are scarce in Australia. Truly natural ones are even more rare. The Aborigines accepted that most water supplies were sporadic: the movements of the animals they hunted, and their own nomadic lives, were ruled by that fact. But European settlers chose accessible rivers and stayed put. They demanded that the water come to them – tamed.

Dams, weirs and levees were built to eliminate the extremes of drought and flood. Banks were straightened and obstacles removed to aid navigation. Flows were diverted to water livestock and irrigate crops. Supplies were drawn off not just for drinking and washing but also for industrial processes, and lately to fill hundreds of thousands of swimming pools.

Even in remote high country, a century or more ago, streams were altered by erosion of their headwater catchments. Forest logging was to blame. More recently, hydro-electric engineering has regulated many rivers, and created new lakes or raised old ones.

Queensland's Barron Falls, once the year-round tourist highlight of the Atherton Tablelands, now flow only in the wet season when the Tinaroo Dam overspills. The Snowy River is deprived of more than 2 million million litres a year by tunnelled diversion to the Murrumbidgee and Murray. The Murray itself is depleted, and salted by the leaching of minerals from cleared land. The Darling, contributing most of the Murray's water, can no longer fluctuate between a chain of billabongs and a flooding sheet hundreds of kilometres wide. Barrages and storage lakes hold it in check.

Where highland rainforests remain untouched, some unspoilt rivers are still to be found flowing in all seasons. Western Tasmania's are the most celebrated – but also the hardest to reach. Many national parks on the Great Dividing Range, however, give access to streams that spill from scarps in waterfalls or cascades, then plunge into ferny ravines.

More indicative of the real nature of most Australian waterways are the braided beds and floodplains of the Channel Country in western Queensland. They are nearly always dry. Even major rivers such as the Diamantina and Cooper Creek are ephemeral, flowing only after prolonged heavy rain. And it takes weeks of the most phenomenal flooding of the Channel Country before the vast salt pans of Lake Eyre are likely to fill.

Monsoon floodplains in the far north are scenes of remarkable annual transformation in plant and animal life. But when it happens, most such districts are inaccessible. The best a traveller can do to appreciate the contrast at Kakadu National Park, for example, is find time for two visits – one just before the wet season, and one as soon as possible after.

Most other national parks in the Northern Terrritory, and all the popular ones to the west from the Kimberleys to Kalbarri, are based on ancient, deeply cut gorges. Their rivers fluctuate seasonally, and in Central Australia most are ephemeral. The attraction for visitors, especially late in the dry season, may be not so much in the watercourses as in the grandeur of their walls. Often the gorges hold pockets of primitive, moist-climate palms and vines – relics of an age long past.

Rivers in the southwest are generally short-flowing and much changed by forest clearance and settlement. Inland, former drainage systems are marked by salt pans, arranged in a horseshoe pattern spanning 500 km. Similar forms extend from north of Lake Eyre to the Flinders Ranges and Eyre Peninsula, SA.

In western NSW, a more recently dried waterway is represented in the Willandra Lakes chain. Mungo National Park's stark lunette walls, like the rims of a moon crater, are built of sands blown from the bed of a lake that held ample water until about 20 000 years ago.

Water storage is so precious now that most natural lakes have been amplified by damming. Australia's deepest, Lake St Clair in Tasmania, was raised to serve power stations on the River Derwent. The greatest of all in area, Lake Argyle in the Kimberleys, was made by damming the Ord River.

Old estuaries, barred by sand ridges, form sizeable coastal lakes in NSW and eastern Victoria. But the streams feeding them are often interfered with, and the lakes themselves modified by settlement or heavy recreational use. Of the few that have been largely spared, outstanding examples are found in The Lakes National Park, Vic, and Myall Lakes National Park, NSW.

The Wimmera River, flowing by Little Desert National Park, gives trees a rare chance in western Victoria

Vast floodplains border the Daly River, NT

THE HIDDEN RESERVOIRS

ARTESIAN water fell as rain – long ago and very far away. It lies under western Queensland and northwestern NSW, and reaches beneath the Central and South Australian deserts. But all of it came from the Eastern Highlands.

The Great Artesian Basin – really a group of basins separated by underground ridges – is a part of Australia that slumped millions of years ago under the weight of inland seas and their deposits. The sediments formed porous rock, to be capped later by impermeable shales. To balance the slumping, land at the eastern rim rose. Wherever the raised edge of the porous layer has been exposed, it has acted as a conduit for rainwater. Moisture seeps down and collects in a water table, sealed underneath by the old sunken rock.

True artesian water bubbles up under its own pressure if the saturated layer is breached. But bore-sinking for almost a century has lowered the water table; pumping is often needed now. The water is increasingly salty as it ages, and it can have a sulphurous, rotten-egg smell. Most of it is used only for livestock. Where it is pumped from great depths it comes up near-boiling, and can be piped for heating.

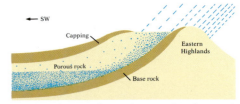

Spongy rock exposed near the Great Divide is sandwiched between layers that water cannot penetrate. Rain sinking into it forms a water table extending more than 1500 km southwestward.

A VICTORY FOR THE WETLANDS

Hundreds of wildlife species rely on shallow inland waters for at least part of each year. Without swamps and marshes, many would be poorly distributed – and some extinct. But the shrinking wetlands remain targets for reclamation or water diversion.

The trend has been reversed in central NSW, where the Macquarie River spreads into 40 000 ha of meandering creeks and reedy marshes west of Coonamble. The marshes are breeding grounds particularly for ibises, along with more than 150 other species of birds and scores of different amphibians, reptiles and fish.

Upstream, the Burrendong Dam regulates the river. After 1969 the flow was sharply reduced while much of the water went to farms. The river petered out in the marshes, which were impoverished year by year.

Early in the 1980s, a proposed expansion of cotton planting called for even more water to be taken off for irrigation. Protesting conservationists were supported by wheatgrowers and graziers, who had learned that the ibis is a major predator of insects that ruin crops and pastures. The state government heeded their call.

Now the flow to the Macquarie Marshes is almost trebled. Waterfowl habitats are fully flooded, and the river can resume its natural course into the Barwon and on into the Lachlan-Darling-Murray system. The marshes, partly declared as nature reserves and listed by the Heritage Commission, are the likely site of a future national park.

Their waters restored, the Macquarie Marshes come back to life

Left: The last run-off from the summer wet season in the Kimberleys, WA, spills into the Prince Regent River. It flows straight for 80 km along a sandstone fracture

Unspoilt waterways meander through The Lakes National Park, Vic, within easy boating distance of popular Gippsland holiday resorts. The lakes were formed out of estuaries, barred by Ninety Mile Beach

THE NATURE OF AUSTRALIA

Where the oceans hold sway

To SEE ALL of Australia's shores at first hand could take a lifetime – or perhaps cost a life. The mainland and Tasmanian coasts, by the most precise measuring method available, extend for more than 30 000 km. Islands on the continental shelf add nearly 18 000 km. Some sections consist of virtually impassable terrain, so far surveyed only from aircraft or boats. Fresh water may not be found for hundreds of kilometres, and the only source of food may be dangerous swamps or seas.

No other country has a coastline so vast, or so pronounced in its contrasts. Shores are backed in some places by deserts, in others by jungles. Towering cliffs and headlands offer seascapes of grandeur; elsewhere the only view may be of mudflats, all the way to the horizon. Ocean currents range from equatorial to subpolar. While seals and Antarctic seabirds breed in the south, warmer waters foster the growth of the world's most massive coral structures.

Australia's coast is noticeably lacking in one respect: for its size, it has very few river outlets. And except near the Eastern Highlands and in the monsoonal north and northwest, rivers have no significant impact on shore formations. There is simply not enough run-off of water or eroded inland rock. Disparity in the supply of material from the hinterland to the coasts, established over millions of years, has led to marked differences in the composition and behaviour of shorelines.

Where plenty of inland material is added to coastal debris, sands are abundant. But they may not stay put. They contain a lot of silica, usually in the form of quartz, so they are slippery. Agitated by waves and winds, they sort themselves until the heaviest minerals – the 'black sands' prized for commercial extraction – lie at the bottom of beaches and dunes. Sands above are light, loose and easily torn away by gales and storm waves.

On arid shores, sands are composed more of marine sediments. Their higher content of shell and skeleton fragments makes them rich in calcium – a binding agent. Blown inland, these sands pile up and consolidate. Many wave-eroded limestone cliffs, reefs and offshore stacks originated as calcified dune ridges, built when the sea level was lower.

Not all parts of the coast are being eroded. Some hold their own against the sea, or even gain ground. Normal wave power is far from uniform around Australia. It is determined by global weather patterns and the breadth and slope of the continental shelf offshore, as well as by local geography. Waves are generally strongest in the south and ineffectual on tropical shores – except in cyclones. In the far north, river silts discharged into quiet shallows are caught in mangroves to make new land.

Wave direction is important, especially to the fate of beaches. Strong waves breaking at an acute angle to a beach create a powerful longshore current. Washed-off sand is carried away parallel to the shoreline. Where this happens consistently, beaches are depleted and the coastline gradually recedes.

Southeasterly winds and waves attack the eastern bulge of the continent with a regularity that makes beach recession a fact of life. Foredune stabilisation and restraints on property development can stop it happening more quickly than necessary, but the process is inevitable. Sand movement up the mid-east coast has been relentless for more than 8000 years, since the sea rose after the last ice age.

The outcome, where the longshore currents weaken at last, is seen in the chain of sand islands off Brisbane, in the richly coloured cliffs north of Noosa, and finally in the huge mass of Fraser Island. Most of the material that built them originated in the Great Dividing Range, perhaps as far south as the Blue Mountains. Similar forces worked on the western seaboard; in almost a mirror image, its old limestone coast is recessed in the south and built out towards the Tropic of Capricorn.

Where strong waves consistently meet a

Coral backs WA's Houtman Abrolhos Islands – once coastal dunes but now 60 km offshore

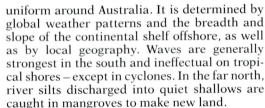

Right: Lime-rich dunes on the Bight near Penong, SA

THE MANGROVE KINGDOM: LIVING WITH THE TIDES

MANGROVES are trees and shrubs of many different kinds, all adapted to daily flooding by sea water. They restrict their intake of salt by chemical action, or get rid of it through their leaves. Their seeds are spread by the tides.

Australia has nearly 50 species. Most are notable for the aerial root systems that help to anchor them in soft mud. In some, the roots have openings through which the trees breathe when their soils are saturated. Other species send up breathing pegs for metres around each tree.

On northern coasts, communities of 20 of more species form broad, dense forests up to 30 metres tall. Diversity and vigour decline farther south. Around Sydney three or four species form open stands, seldom exceeding 15 metres. In Victoria, South Australia and south of Perth there is only the grey mangrove, stunted and sparsely distributed.

Boat users and resort developers may see mangroves as nuisances. But they stabilise shorelines by trapping silt in their tangled roots. And their fallen leaves start an estuarine food chain on which marine animals – including most commercially harvested fish – depend. Each square metre of tropical mangrove forest yields about 1 kg of organic matter every year.

Silt collects in a tropical tangle

shore head-on, they can add to the land. They push sand in to form nearshore barriers, sometimes shutting off bays or estuaries. The lagoons that are created eventually fill with silts and windblown sands. Beaches formed of massive barriers occur frequently on the east coast between the Tropic and Wilsons Promontory, and are also found in eastern South Australia and south of Perth.

Tropical Queensland and the Northern Territory, with weaker wave action, have lower barrier beaches less obvious in their origin. Gulfs and landlocked bays in these regions tend to fill as tidal mudflats, backed by broad mangrove beds and salt marshes and sometimes fringed with coral. Open tidal plains, reaching for many kilometres between high and low waterlines, occur widely on each side of North West Cape between Shark Bay and Port Hedland.

Long, open mainland beaches, free of barriers, develop where the general direction of waves is past a shoreline rather than at it. Reefs and rocky sections may give protection, but the sandy stretches predominate. They are common in western Victoria and northern and eastern Tasmania, towards the head of the Bight and in some parts of the southwest.

Headlands interrupt most beach coasts in the southeast, giving shelter and good vantage points. Their bases usually have wave-cut shore platforms, teeming with marine life. Continuously cliffed coasts, however, are rare. The principal ones in accessible areas are immediately south of Sydney – through Royal National Park and beyond – in Otway and Port Campbell National Parks in Victoria, and around most of southeastern Tasmania.

Sheer limestone cliffs give a sharp edge to much of the Nullarbor Plain, and to the desolate western extremity of the continent, north of Kalbarri National Park. The longest rock coast of all skirts the Kimberleys, where red sandstone precipices are cut by fiordlike inlets. Prodigious tides that can range up to 12 metres create channelled currents of freakish violence. And tidal bores – waves that race up rivers – can overturn boats 50 km inland.

Often it is the reefs and islands offshore that most distinguish a coast. They enrich its scenic variety, and give sanctuary to animals and plants rarely seen on the mainland. In spite of Australia's extreme emphasis on seaboard settlement and maritime recreation, landing problems and a lack of fresh water saved many islands. Now an impressive number are fully protected as nature reserves. Others rank among our most celebrated national parks.

Remote island parks, with a controlled flow of visitors, are easily managed. But on closer islands – especially the Queensland islands with fringing coral – the risks of damage are high. The jeopardy of the reef at Green Island, off Cairns, prompted a marine park declaration. That concept of below-the-waterline protection is now applied in defence of almost all of the Great Barrier Reef region.

A scalloped beach line, seen strikingly at Safety Cove on Tasman Peninsula, Tas, results when incoming and receding waves collide and set up an eddying pattern. On a surfing beach, it may indicate dangerous rip currents

The Drum and Drumsticks, off Beecroft Peninsula, NSW, are remnants of an older coastline

THE NATURE OF AUSTRALIA
The eternal battle of the trees

PLANTS CANNOT RUN from hostile conditions. To survive, they must adapt and diversify. In Australia they have answered with an explosion of species. Flowering plants alone number about 11 000 kinds, from tiny herbs to towering eucalypts. Mosses, ferns, fungi and cone-bearing trees add to the array. And rivalry is intense. Plants struggle not only against climatic setbacks, animal appetites and human ambitions, but also against one another.

The story of land vegetation starts well over 400 million years ago. Leafless, branching strands of a mossy seaweed crept ashore from the intertidal zone and invaded swamps and marshes. Adapting to more and more exposure to the air, the plants evolved into mosses and colonised firm ground.

Root systems were developed to tap subsurface water. Plants with thick, rigid stems appeared – the ancestors of ferns, club-mosses and horsetails. Competing for light, they reached up on ever-stronger trunks and became the first trees. Forests grew widely, dominated by club-mosses 30 metres tall. Coal deposits are their petrified remains.

Next, more than 250 million years ago, came the conifers – pine trees and their relatives. They broke away from reliance on ground water to disperse reproductive spores; their pollen is produced high in the tree, to be scattered by winds. Another cone-bearing group, short-trunked cycads with palmlike or fernlike fronds, appeared at about the same time. Pines and cycads ruled until 80-90 million years ago.

Flowering plants were taking over by then, especially in warmer climates. Their vivid petals, alluring scents and nectar drew insects, ensuring a more effective transfer of pollen. Magnolias and figs were among the pioneers, and beeches gained early prominence in forests. Palms were soon abundant, and took many forms. The striking thing about the flowering plants was how quickly they produced variations to suit different soils and climates.

The realm of the conifers had been worldwide. But continental isolation was setting in when flowering plants came to the fore. Africa had separated from the southern supercontinent of Gondwanaland, and India and South America were in the process of breaking away. After New Zealand drifted off, about 80 million years ago, Australia's only neighbour – and source of new plants – was Antarctica.

In the last phase of separation, some 60 million years ago, southern Australia and Antarctica shared cool-climate rainforests. Conifers still predominated, among an increasing variety of flowering trees including some beeches. Almost nothing is known of the vegetation of inland and northern Australia, but it can be assumed that the forerunners of nearly all of today's species were established. The only important exceptions, in the far north, came much later from Asia through New Guinea.

Australia's breach with Antarctica was completed about 55 million years ago. The continent began its journey northwestward into warmer latitudes. But world temperatures generally were falling, and patterns of atmospheric circulation changing. Land upheavals and sea incursions modified climates and soils in the east and south. Browsing and grazing mammals and seed-eating birds spread. But plant evolution went on. Now in isolation, it took paths that were to create a uniquely Australian bush.

With the first uplift of the Eastern Highlands completed, about 45 million years ago, beech rainforests entered a long period of dominance

Pencil pine grows only in alpine Tasmania

BUILT BY PRIMITIVE PLANTS

CLUMPS like soft rock jut from sand and mud at Hamelin Pool, a shallow arm of Shark Bay, WA. In deeper water they stand in columns up to 3 metres tall. Found in thousands, these are living colonies of single-celled plants bound by secretions of lime.

The microscopic plants, called cyanophytes, represent the earliest form of life after bacteria – and the first to put oxygen into the air. They grow commonly in mats, like algae, and are usually grazed by molluscs. Only at Hamelin Pool are they left alone to build. The outlet is choked, and high evaporation makes the water too salty for molluscs.

Shorn-off cyanophyte mounds, solidified in silica, are found as big white rings in ancient rocks all over the world. Before their organic origin was known they were named stromatolites – 'mattress stones'. Some were built by plants growing 3000 million years ago.

Oddities of western and northern WA: Millstream palms (left) and baobabs or bottle trees – called boabs by locals

at least in the south. The general climate was still moist, but the interior of the continent was already more arid. And plants there were adapting. Trees that had emerged in luxury, enjoying abundant rainfall and rich soils, differentiated to include hardier forms.

Out of the acacia family – the wattles – came an exclusively Australian type with flattened, thornlike stems instead of leaves. From the myrtles, which in tropical America bear a soft, pulpy fruit, came eucalypts with tough, woody capsules. Both groups are thought to have gained some prominence in open forests by 30 million years ago. They and many other flowering trees continued to vary, developing scrubbier forms to survive in the poorest soils.

No one knows when the first alien plants may have arrived, their seeds carried by ocean currents or migratory birds. But intermittently over the past 10 million years, since Australia came into close contact with New Guinea, invaders of Southeast Asian origin have travelled overland. They established themselves with particular success in northern rainforests.

In most of the south, also about 10 million years ago, beech forests suddenly gave way to eucalypts. Some open woodlands and grasslands appeared, though their major expansion did not occur until 3-1 million years ago. By then the world was entering a period – continuing now – in which the climate fluctuated in cycles of glaciation and heating.

Trees advanced or retreated according to their resistance to frost, heat and drought – and increasingly to fire. Expanding populations of browsing animals chewed at them. Through it all, the grasses gained ground. They carpeted alpine plateaux and semi-arid plains, and clung in hummocks in places so barren that not even the scrub eucalypts and acacias could survive.

In a climate steadily more arid, rainforests

Cycads ruled for eons before palms evolved

were forced back to the eastern margins of the continent about 2 million years ago. Since then, in patches within those limits, they have contracted and expanded many times in a to-and-fro struggle with dry-adapted trees. And in tropical rainforests, the component plants have fought among themselves. Different species show up during each phase of resurgence, in fossils taken from the same spot.

Fire has been a powerful influence on Australian plant evolution for many millions of years. The fact that so many species benefit from burning and some even rely on it is evidence of that. But charcoal deposits and soil studies show a marked increase in the frequency of fires – and the expansion of grasslands – in the past 40 000 years.

Aborigines used fire to foster the wildlife they hunted. Blazes were started judiciously to keep woodlands clear of litter and encourage grass growth – not too often, yet not so seldom that huge conflagrations were caused. But European settlers anxious for agricultural land burned forests, woodlands and scrublands indiscriminately, and their raging fires bared far more ground than was needed.

Rainforest logging, the substitution of exotic plantations and the spread of introduced pasture grasses and farm crops have all had an obvious impact on native vegetation. More subtle is the conversion of soils by compaction under the hooves of thousands of millions of livestock. Often the bush is damaged by feral animals such as goats and pigs, or supplanted by alien trees and weeds. But on the vast scale of plant evolution, all these are just further complications – and perhaps passing phases – in a battle that never ends.

THE NATURE OF AUSTRALIA

Rainforests: a squandered heritage

Scores of tree species vie for space and light in the one small patch of tropical rainforest

RAINFORESTS are the scattered relics of an ancient time when most of Australia was moist and fertile. Driven back by a drying climate, they were overtaken by trees better able to resist drought and fire. Before Europeans came, the domain of rainforests was reduced already to less than 1 per cent of the continent's area. Now it is barely a quarter of that. In the main, whatever was most accessible has gone.

Generations of loggers and farmers who felled or burned the trees were largely ignorant of the consequences. They did not realise the extent to which they would trigger off soil erosion and the loss of water yields. They could not foresee a day when the forests would be needed to purify a polluted atmosphere. Least of all could they have understood that they were depleting a genetic store in which some stock – perhaps unseen – might be unique.

Even today it is not always grasped that rainforest species are interdependent. A certain tree may be widely distributed, so its removal from one forest seems harmless. But that could spell the doom of other plants whose habitat is more limited. Simply letting too much light in can kill many species. They may be merely fungi or mosses of no apparent significance. But they could have undiscovered properties important to human survival.

Shade – not just wetness or the types of trees – makes a rainforest. The leaves of the taller trees intermingle to form a canopy. By most botanical definitions, rainforests are at least 70 per cent enclosed under their canopies. Some are totally closed: treetops cannot be seen from the ground, and any light is filtered. Such forests are so humid that hot weather is intolerable – and so dark that walkers may be unable to see hazards.

Left alone, a rainforest recycles the mineral nutrients in dead trees and other fallen material. Decay is so rapid that the soil need not be especially fertile – nearly all the nutrients are stored above ground. But if erosion strips off the litter, or it is burnt and the ash washes away, the forest starves. So the local occurrence of rainforests is related not only to rainfall reliability but also to the least likelihood of fire. Even where eucalypts have come to rule, pockets of rainforest survive in protected gorges and gullies.

Tasmania has the most extensive rainforests – cool spreads of myrtle beech richly carpeted with mosses and ferns. They also occur in limited areas of Victoria. Stands of the closely related negrohead beech occupy high ranges in northern NSW and southern Queensland. Ancestors of these beeches were established before the southern supercontinent of Gondwanaland broke up: kindred trees grow in New Zealand and Chile and are fossilised in Antarctica. Later, beeches were probably the commonest forest trees in most of Australia.

Beech forests are simple in composition. Mature stands grow to a uniform height and have no understoreys made up of other tree species. Tree ferns may grow luxuriantly where the canopy is more open – particularly along riverbanks. But the forest floors are mainly mossy. Epiphytes – plants that attach themselves to others – and parasites, which feed off

Left: Cool-temperate forests of myrtle beech grow widely in Tasmania and in patches in Victoria – such as this one in Wilsons Promontory National Park. Tree ferns abound where the canopy opens along rivers

Negrohead beech, the ruler of temperate rainforests, near the northern end of its range in Nightcap National Park, NSW

others, are few except for lichens. The beeches may grow to 30 metres, but in the coldest conditions do not exceed 10 metres.

Northern rainforests are much more complex. More than 100 different tree species may be found in one hectare, and none is noticeably dominant. The general height of the canopy is usually 30 metres or so, but here and there an emergent tree stands much taller. And below the canopy are understoreys of shorter trees. Vines climb towards the light, and epiphytes such as orchids and staghorn and elkhorn ferns are abundant. But the forest floor is surprisingly open. Palms and ferns grow fairly sparsely among fleshy-leafed herbs and a few small shrubs and tree seedlings. These seedlings seem never to get any taller – but if adult trees come down, through old age or storm damage, the opening of the canopy brings them shooting up to fill the gap.

Lichen-covered and nearly always buttressed at their bases, the different northern trees are hard to tell apart at ground level. Prized timber species surviving in remote forests include red cedar, coachwood, silky oak, Queensland maple and teak and the imposing kauri, which reaches 50 metres. This great pine, with relatives in New Zealand and New Caledonia, has a lineage even older than the beeches. The northern forests are equally a part of the Gondwanaland legacy.

Forests in the far north have been enriched more recently, however, by Asiatic plants arriving through New Guinea. That heightens a distinction often made between tropical and subtropical northern rainforests. The first kind contain many more species. But the division has nothing to do with the line of the Tropic of Capricorn – it relates to temperature ranges and altitude. Tropical forests in this sense are not found south of Townsville, and even to the north they are replaced by subtropical mixtures in the higher country.

The northern half of Cape York Peninsula has part-time rainforests. Plants here have to cope with months of drought between monsoons. So the forests are dominated by deciduous species that conserve moisture by shedding their leaves at the onset of the dry season. Since roads are open only in the 'Dry', most travellers do not recognise the rainforests. Small patches of similar vegetation occur in the Darwin region, where they are more often called monsoon vineforests.

Beyond their scenic value and their importance as botanical storehouses, rainforests are the busiest havens of wildlife on land. They seethe with the activities of myriads of creatures, at every level from the leaf litter to the topmost flower heads. Rare insects, amphibians, mammals and birds are among the occupants. Whatever threatens rainforests may ring the death knell of these animals.

Starting life as seeds lodged high in other tropical trees, curtain figs send down prop roots – then strangle their hosts

THE PARKS WHERE RAINFORESTS RULE

Pockets of rainforest are found in the majority of eastern national parks. Those areas with a significant amount of rainforest include:

Cairns region Barron Gorge, Bellenden Ker, Cape Tribulation, Clump Mountain (Maria Creek group), Daintree, Dunk Island, Ella Bay, Graham Range, Green Island, Grey Peaks, Iron Range, Lake Barrine, Lake Eacham, Lizard Island, Mount Hypipamee, Palmerston group, Topaz Road, Tully Gorge.

Townsville region Conway, Eungella, Goold Island (Hinchinbrook Island group), Jourama, Lumholtz, Mount Jukes (Mount Blackwood group), Mount Spec, Orpheus Island, Whitsunday Island.

Rockhampton region Cape Palmerston, Coalstoun Lakes, Fairlies Knob (Mount Walsh group), Kroombit Tops, Mount Bauple, Northumberland Islands.

Brisbane region Bunya Mountains, Burleigh Head, Conondale, Lamington, Maiala (D'Aguilar Range group), Main Range, Springbrook, Tamborine Mountain group, The Palms.

NSW northern border region Border Ranges, Dorrigo, Gibraltar Range, Mount Warning, New England, Nightcap, Washpool.

Melbourne region Alfred, Tarra-Bulga, Croajingolong, Mitchell River, Otway, Wilsons Promontory.

Tasmania Cradle Mountain-Lake St Clair, Mount Field, Southwest, Walls of Jerusalem, Franklin-Gordon Wild Rivers.

THE NATURE OF AUSTRALIA
The forests that welcome fire

TREES MEET nature's harshest terms in Australia's open forests and woodlands. They face the certainty of wildfire. Many have adapted so that they can recover after burning. And some – particularly the eucalypts – now depend on fire for their procreation. They give typical 'gum tree' bushland not only its own look but even its own smell: evaporating oils.

Long before humans arrived to step up the pace of destruction, fires occurred naturally. Lightning strikes were most often the cause. The trees that stood the best chance were those with lignotubers – swellings near the base of the trunk containing latent buds. These come to life if the tree is damaged above. In some species lignotubers are seen as warty lumps on the trunk. But many Australian trees have them underground, extending much like roots.

Eucalypts and some of their companion trees in the open forests developed further defences. They enclosed their seeds in woody cases instead of soft fruits, and many acquired unusually thick bark. But the most successful species went beyond mere survival – they found ways of exploiting fire for their own benefit. They made sure that when a forest was burnt out, it was replaced by their offspring rather than an invading species. Evolution has brought some eucalypts to a point at which, once at least in their seed-bearing lives, they *need* burning down.

The tallest and fastest-growing eucalypts occupy high-rainfall districts. But they rely on strong light. If an overgrown forest becomes too shady, eucalypt seedlings are killed by fungi. Such a forest is waiting for a dry spell followed by a hot, fast-moving fire. Then, at the height of its destruction, it re-seeds itself.

Fed by streamers of peeling bark, flames race up the trunks to the forest canopy. Vaporised leaf oil ignites – sometimes it explodes – drawing the fire even more quickly away from the ground and through the canopy. And from under the vanishing foliage pours a shower of seed capsules – the output of not just one season, but perhaps three or four.

If the fire has moved on quickly enough the seeds are undamaged. (In a furnace test, green capsules protected their seeds for 9 minutes at 440°C.) Germination starts in a bed of ash, holding mineral nutrients in a form that the seedlings can most readily absorb. Their growth is astonishing: some saplings gain 5 metres in a year. In a burnt eucalypt forest, trees of other families have no chance of taking over.

Tall open forests – referred to in older books as wet hardleaf or wet sclerophyll forests – are at their most grand in the extreme southeast and southwest. In Tasmania and Victoria they include the world's tallest hardwood, mountain ash *Eucalyptus regnans*, which can exceed 100 metres. In Western Australia the karri *Eucalyptus diversicolor*, only slightly shorter, is king. Alpine ash, brown stringybark, blackbutt and blue gum are prominent in NSW, and rose gum is characteristic around Brisbane.

These forests are more open at the top than rainforests – canopy coverage is 30-70 per cent – but much leafier below. There is always a dense understorey of shorter eucalypt species and taller shrubs. On rich soils in the moistest areas, some of the understorey plants are rainforest species – on the way to taking over if fire does not come. With tree ferns, lichens and epiphytes abundant, some wet open forests at ground level look much like rainforests. But the trunk bases are not buttressed.

The dominion of eucalypts continues in drier open forests in southern Australia but the trees seldom exceed 30 metres. Fires are more frequent and most species are adapted to resist, then recover through lignotubers. Understoreys are less leafy, with acacias, casuarinas and banksias usually prominent. The most characteristic eucalypt species include peppermint, bloodwood, scribbly gum, stringybark and 'apple' (angophora) in the southeast, and

Heartwood fire dooms a tree – but its scattered seeds and underground tubers are intact

Damage higher up triggers new growth from a charred trunk

Left: A handsome stand of marri, with an understorey of karri oak, in WA's Walpole-Nornalup National Park. Marri grows widely in the southwest where it reaches heights of 30-40 metres. It shares the same range as jarrah and karri and often occurs with them. Its timber does not compare with that of the other two hardwoods – it is marred by gum pockets and rings

DIEBACK: SHARING THE BLAME

COUNTLESS diseases and pests attack eucalypts – especially where natural balances are disrupted. If large numbers of trees are slowly dying, their decline is generally labelled 'dieback'. It is not one problem but many, with different causes.

A soil-borne fungus attacks the giant jarrahs of Western Australia. To limit its spread some state forest areas and national parks are quarantined; there are wash-down facilities to prevent vehicles carrying infected soil from one area to another; road construction and use are restricted.

Dieback in irrigation areas (particularly in the Murray-Murrumbidgee Basin) occurs because of salting and an altered water table: too much water prevents soil aeration and rots tree roots; too little and the trees die of thirst.

Leaf-eating Christmas beetles and other insects are a major cause of eucalypt dieback in the New England district of NSW. Development of pastoral agriculture has provided more food for the beetles' larval stage while removing farmland trees so there are fewer birds to eat increasing numbers of beetles.

River red gum dieback in northwestern Victoria

In the Dandenong Ranges near Melbourne, the problem seems to be too many birds. Dieback has occurred in about 10 per cent of the forest cover because of an infestation by sap-sucking insects called psyllids. These are husbanded by a big population of bellbirds, which eat only the older psyllids and encourage the young to develop. Other birds with less selective appetites are driven away.

messmate, boxes and pink gum near Adelaide. The Perth region has its own group, dominated by jarrah, marri and wandoo.

Casuarinas and acacias rule in many open forests in Queensland, between hoop pine on the wetter seaward margins and cypress pine at the inland limit of forest growth. There are also some eucalypt forests, with grassy floors suggesting that they gained their hold through firing by Aboriginal hunters. Similar grassy eucalypt forests occur in the Darwin region and the Kimberleys, and along the Murray River Valley where they are dominated by the flood-loving river red gum.

Woodlands are distinguished from forests by having a canopy coverage of less than 30 per cent of their area. Often they are simply extensions of forest communities, more widely spaced because they have less soil moisture to share. Grasses are much more common, however. And some non-eucalypt species – melaleucas (paperbarks), for example – take on a prominence not seen in forests. Brigalow, once the most significant of woodland acacias, exists now only in remnants on its range from inland mid-Queensland to northern NSW.

In woodlands as much as in forests, eucalypts remain the most widespread and dominant trees. Their forms range from the snow gums of alpine summits to monsoon species that shed their leaves for the 'Dry'. Counting the stunted types of the outback, there may be more than 500 eucalypt species; botanists are forever making new finds and classifications,

Tree ferns are characteristic of the cooler wet eucalypt forests of the southeast – but never found in those of the west

and raising or lowering the figure. However many there are, eucalypts represent the plant kingdom's greatest evolutionary triumph – a conquest of every climatic extreme that the continent can offer.

But the unmistakable aroma of 'gum' leaves, and the blue haze pervading forests in hot weather, are reminders of menace. The layers of oily foliage and the thickly littered floors are incendiary bombs, certain sooner or later to go off. Eucalypts and many of their companions have accommodated to an element against which humans are largely helpless. Fire is a fact of their lives.

25

THE NATURE OF AUSTRALIA
Sentinels of the never-never

SCRUB, SPINIFEX and saltbush ... half of Australia is dismissed in three words. Yet in some ways the vegetation of the scorched, parched outback is the most important of all. It sustained the spread of Aboriginal tribes. It afforded the food, shelter and fuel to make the continent traversable – if seldom habitable – by Europeans and their livestock. And in spite of these intrusions, it has ensured the survival of many wildlife species.

Hardly any of the hinterland is absolute desert. Almost anywhere something grows, to make up the world's greatest array of dry-living plants. But two groups of stunted trees, mulga and mallee, have a hold so persistent that their habitats take their names. The Mulga is an immense tract of acacia scrub and sparse shrubland sweeping across Western Australia into the Northern Territory and South Australia, with outliers to the east. The Mallee's parched plains span southwestern NSW, northwestern Victoria and eastern South Australia. Even more mallee country extends west of Adelaide and round the Great Australian Bight to beyond Kalgoorlie, WA.

Mulga denotes one main wattle species, *Acacia aneura*, which on the best soils can reach 15 metres but in its shrub form can be as low as 2 metres. Its many branches, rising steeply from the ground or just above, carry slightly flattened stems – called phyllodes – instead of leaves. These have a hairy, resinous covering and point skyward to minimise heating. Trees go dormant in drought, but revive within four days of receiving moisture in their soil. They do best where there is some chance of rain at any time of year; in regions of strongly seasonal rainfall they tend to be replaced by casuarinas – the so-called oaks.

Aboriginal boomerangs and many souvenir ornaments are made of mulga wood. Livestock prefer browsing the phyllodes – though they are not particularly nutritious – to eating dry grass. Mulga is harvested as emergency fodder in droughts, and sometimes cleared where there is an understorey of edible tussock grasses. But the trees are secure in the driest areas, and where their understoreys are of inedible small shrubs or hummock grasses.

Mallees are ground-branching eucalypts. More than 100 species have been identified. They form a spreading bush, usually 3-9 metres tall, from an underground lignotuber that contains latent buds to regenerate the tree if it is damaged. Six months after a fire, they may have produced up to 70 new shoots. Stem branches are few and leaves are borne only at the tips of the branches. In dense scrub they form a distinctive canopy cover, shallow and almost horizontal.

Since drought-resistant wheat strains were developed, extensive mallee areas have been cleared – with some calamitous consequences. Without the cover of the mallees and their understorey shrubs and grasses, strong winds after long dry spells can rip all of the topsoil away. Millions of tonnes of red dust are dumped in choking storms on towns and cities or into the oceans; some is even blown as far as New Zealand.

On limy or salty soils, both mulga and mallee may merge into country dominated by low chenopod shrubs – saltbushes and their relatives. They are palatable to stock, and when agriculture invaded the outback their territories were the easiest to take. Saltbushes decline with years of grazing: of about 250 chenopod species, more than 20 are expected to disappear from the wild by the end of the century. But the others hold about 6 per cent of the mainland area. Most are in inland South Australia and on the Nullarbor Plain, with an isolated stronghold in western NSW around the dried-out Willandra Lakes.

Spiky hummock grasses dot arid land over a quarter of the continent, from the northwest coast into Queensland and south almost to the Nullarbor. Mostly species of *Triodia*, they are usually called spinifex – though true *Spinifex* exists as a coastal sand-binding plant. To avoid confusion some people call the inland hummock type porcupine grass. It normally occurs in mulga scrub or casuarina woodlands, but on rocky slopes and sandplains it may provide the only ground cover.

Open grasslands of softer, edible tussocks such as Mitchell grass range from south of Arnhem Land and the Gulf of Carpentaria to southwestern Queensland. But most are heavily grazed. Untouched grasslands now are vir-

Spinifex and snappy gums on the Hamersley Range, WA

Poached-egg daisies: the waiting is over

PLANTS THAT HIDE FROM DROUGHT

RAIN in late winter changes the look of arid inland regions with remarkable speed. Unseen in the ground are seeds that can bide their time through years of drought. When conditions favour them they burst into hectic life. Plants shoot in hours and flower in days. Almost as quickly they wither and die, leaving a new generation of seeds to wait once more.

Most such plants – called ephemerals – are members of the daisy or pea families. Their seeds are programmed so as not to be fooled by a passing shower, or by heavier rain at the wrong time of year. As well as searing heat, frost must be avoided. Germination is triggered only by a certain combination of moisture, temperature and light intensity.

Ephemerals have their easiest life near rock outcrops, where they may flourish annually in pockets of run-off moisture. In Central Australia, the seepage of dew from sealed, high-crowned highways is sometimes enough to promote growth along a narrow band at each side. But the most spectacular shows follow heavy rains on flat country. Drab tonings turn green, then explode into vivid colours as far as the eye can see.

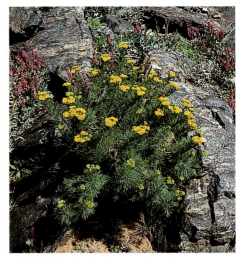

Hops and everlastings make the most of run-off

but most do not need to. Their seeds are distributed whenever they are ready – by harvester ants. These seeds all have a tough casing but they bear a soft tail. The ants carry the seeds to their nests, eat the tail, then discard the seeds undamaged. Sometimes they store them in underground galleries. Some 1500 Australian plant species use ants in this fashion, compared with fewer than 300 anywhere else in the world.

Heathlands in the east and south are generally small patches, merging into scrub or woodlands. Most are coastal, on sandy soils. But highland heaths occur in parts of the Great Dividing Range – on soils derived from sandstone or granite – and in Tasmania. In the west, immense tracts of heathland reach east from Albany and north from Kalbarri – not merely along the coast but also on sandplains well inland. It is their predominance that gives Western Australia its well-justified reputation as 'the wildflower state'.

Left: Mallees and pearl bluebush – a kind of saltbush – merge on the sandplains of Nullarbor National Park, SA. Feral camels are often seen

Below: Scrubs at Wyperfeld National Park, Vic, support at least 200 native bird species

tually confined to very wet areas – the high buttongrass plains of southwestern Tasmania, for example, or the swampgrass plains near parts of the NSW south coast.

Heathland plants make up the remainder of the vegetation of the wide-open spaces. In their domain, forest growth is ruled out not by aridity but by soil infertility. In compensation, the flowering shrubs of the heathlands present the most vivid scenes of the bush, and support a profusion of wildlife. Birds such as honeyeaters and parrots are likeliest to catch the eye, but smaller marsupials also feed on nectar and on the insects that swarm in the undergrowth.

Australia's main family of true heaths, the epacrids, has more than 300 species. The best known, common heath with its dangling tubular flowers borne year-round, is Victoria's floral emblem. Lilies and their relatives grow mostly as heath plants, along with thousands of smaller flowering species including ground orchids in a rich variety of forms and colours. But they and the true heaths are dominated by mixtures of taller woody shrubs. The most characteristic family, the proteaceae, includes banksias, grevilleas, hakeas, waratahs and Western Australia's dryandras. Small eucalypts, acacias, paperbarks, tea-trees and casuarinas are also common – but often the most distinctive plants of heathlands are grass trees.

Nearly all species on the fire-prone heathlands can regenerate from underground organs. Some release seed capsules during a fire,

PART TWO
Parks and people

Simple pleasures in a delightful setting: Walyunga National Park on the outskirts of Perth

Running a national park is a balancing act — protecting the environment while letting people enjoy it. Each place has its special problems, with dedicated rangers and backroom staff working to solve them. But a great deal more is up to the public.

PARKS AND PEOPLE

Why we have national parks

TAXPAYERS' MONEY goes into national parks, so people are entitled to see some return for it. Where parks provide recreational opportunities close to cities, or where they preserve unusually spectacular scenery, the benefits are clear. The value of protecting wildlife habitats is also widely recognised at last. But in an increasing number of cases, the worth of new parks is far from obvious to the public.

Some are dedicated in places that no one but a scientist would dream of visiting. Western Australia's vast Rudall River National Park, for example, covers a forbidding expanse of rock ridges and dunes between the Gibson and Great Sandy Deserts. It has no roads, and seldom any water. Many parks are sited in high country so rugged that it is penetrated only by expert climbers. Others occupy monotonous stretches of scrub or swampland, offering nothing noteworthy to see or do.

Public benefits are derived in indirect and sometimes unexpected ways. The real importance of a high, forested park may lie in ensuring the adequacy and purity of water supplies to a nearby community. Even without rain, trees shed more moisture than they receive from the air. And they combat air pollution.

Apart from the varying scenic and recreational merits of national parks, and their role in the protection of the environment and wildlife, they can offer four other advantages from which the whole community stands to gain:

Education Field studies by school groups and trainee teachers are given active assistance. Junior ranger programmes encourage children to follow nature interests in their spare time. Advice by parks staff is also offered in courses for private landowners.

Scientific research Professional studies and experiments are permitted in national parks if they cannot be mounted elsewhere and are not unduly destructive. Untouched areas also serve as models, against which scientists can measure what happens when similar environments outside the parks are interfered with.

Biological banks Without park protection, many plants and animals would no longer exist. Their genetic combinations would be lost to the world. So would the possibility of using them to develop new medicines, food sources and industrial techniques.

Foreign income The fame of many of Australia's national parks is a powerful magnet to overseas visitors. And a major export earner, the fishing industry, depends on the protection of estuarine and island breeding grounds.

If planners had unlimited funds, they would provide many more parks. In the meantime, where population pressures are intense, they encourage passive recreation. They want visitors to relax, look and listen, rather than seek too many artificial amenities and active pastimes. Popular enjoyment has to be balanced against the fragility of natural environments – or else there may be nothing to enjoy later on.

Park administrations bear a responsibility to future generations, not only in Australia but also throughout the world. Our parks and wildlife services belong to an international union, formed under United Nations auspices, and the federal and state governments endorse all of its ideals. But we struggle to live up to them.

The international convention calls for national parks and nature reserves to make up at least 5 per cent of any country's territory. Australia, in spite of many recent additions, falls far short. And the parks are meant to represent every kind of biological community. Again Australia fails: virtually all temperate and subtropical grasslands, for example, have long been transformed by livestock.

Scarcity of land puts environmental aims in conflict with industrial interests. Remaining areas suitable for parks are often earmarked for mining or logging or hydro-electricity generation. Political pressures to continue indus-

Scientists are still exploring at Rudall River, WA. The public's turn will come much later

Schoolchildren find an easy introduction to nature study at Ferntree Gully National Park, Vic

trial activity, at least for a time, are usually intense. Sometimes a mixture of uses seems entirely reasonable. But the international agreement requires a nation's 'highest competent authority' to eliminate any exploitation in national parks.

Australia's trouble has been that the highest authority, the federal government, holds absolute power only in Commonwealth territories – the ACT, the Northern Territory, Jervis Bay and some remote oceanic islands. Elsewhere, the federal system gives state governments the right to declare their own reserves and dispose of them as they please. Their older 'national' parks were created under diverse political influences to achieve different goals. Nationwide concerns were never paramount – let alone international responsibilities.

Dissension over such issues as uranium mining, oil prospecting and civil engineering continues to make political battlegrounds of some present and proposed national parks. But in management techniques and planning, at least, Canberra and the states are now in closer accord. Since the mid-1970s all legislatures have passed national parks and wildlife acts along broadly similar lines. Under a council of all the ministers with nature conservation responsibilities, senior officials of the various parks services form a standing committee to co-ordinate policies.

All of Australia's governments today have the benefit of the same high grade of professional advice on nature conservation, considered in the full light of national need. None of them wishes to be seen as environmentally irresponsible, so recommendations for new or expanded parks are usually received sympathetically. Whether enough money can be found to manage them, and provide the right balance of protection and public enjoyment, is altogether another matter.

The Royal: where it all started

Park expansion at Era took in holiday shacks – and herds of imported deer

IDEAS of nature conservation took a back seat in 1879, when Australia's first national park was conceived. The vision was not of a noble wilderness, to be kept sacred, but of a tamed and groomed playground – a Sydney version of London's Hampstead Heath.

Creation of the National Park (its only name for three-quarters of a century) was primarily a public health measure. Sydney's population had doubled in a decade: in some slums, one child in four died before it was five years old. The people needed common land.

Country to the south, cut off by the Hacking River, was about to be opened up by the Illawarra railway. Legislators reserved 7000 hectares for public recreation, and trustees hastened to meet the leisure tastes of the time. Riverside forest was hacked down to make way for lawns and European trees. Deer were brought in, and exotic birds and fish were released. A causeway controlled the river. Pavilions, guest houses and camps sprang up nearby. Cart roads and bridle paths wound into the bush. A tourist village, Audley, had its own vegetable plots, dairy pastures, orchard and blacksmith's forge.

Sports grounds were envisaged – even a horse racing track. In the meantime, undeveloped areas were cleared by the army for manoeuvres and artillery practice. And to recoup the cost of public amenities, the trustees were allowed to license grazing, logging and mining in the park.

Nature lovers were objecting before World War I, and in 1922 they successfully challenged a mining company's right to fell and mill native trees for pit props. But they could do nothing to stem the tide of cars that soon started to swamp the park. The trustees saw it as their duty to provide maximum access.

Motor roads criss-crossed the heathlands and reached the coastal cliffs and bays. People parked, picnicked, camped and cut firewood anywhere. Beach shacks appeared, and during the 1930s Depression the railway side of the park was dotted with humpies put up by jobless men. Some made livings by stealing greenery to supply city florists, or by selling cartloads of timber or soil.

Still more bush suffered in World War II, when the army set up coastal defences and used much of the park for training exercises. Postwar affluence brought a new flood of cars and motor bikes, and the first 'scrub bashers' in off-road vehicles.

The park was granted its Royal prefix in 1955, but to conservationists it seemed a lost cause. Still, it served as an object lesson, readily pointed to by professional ecologists when official policies came under fire in the next decade. After NSW set up Australia's first integrated parks and wildlife service in 1967, the professionals took charge of the mutilated old reserve and set about giving it another chance.

Cars were restricted to a few formed roads and parking zones. Ramshackle buildings were demolished. Maintenance of ornamental gardens and any other attempts to outdo nature were abandoned. The bush came back, season by season, until in its centenary year at the end of the 1970s the Royal National Park could wear its title with some pride.

Imitating an English pleasure garden suited Sydney ideas of ease in Edwardian times

Soldiers took over in World War I, baring the heathlands

PARKS AND PEOPLE

Jacks and Jills of all trades

OUTDOOR WORK in a pleasant setting ... that is one part of the picture of a park ranger's life. But another may be writing reports and keeping financial records – or cleaning lavatories. Some tasks entail days and nights of utter solitude. Others require the poise and patience to deal with constant streams of people. Physical demands are high. Rangers have to be dedicated, fit and above all versatile.

Looking after the public constitutes the major part of the workload. Visitors expect easy road access and parking. They want eating facilities, campsites, piped water and sanitation – and nobody else's garbage. They seek information: signposts, leaflets, displays, advice. And they are entitled to safety. Walking routes must be secured and waterways patrolled. People astray in big parks may have to be found and helped, and perhaps given first-aid treatment. But all too often, what park visitors need most is policing.

Enforcement of regulations is the priority role of all rangers. They must keep dogs, cats and firearms out of parks, and make sure that no native plants, animals, rocks or soil are taken without licence. They must try to prevent off-road driving, and any intrusion into areas that are quarantined because plants are regenerating or endangered animals are breeding. Vitally, they have to see that fire restrictions and bans are obeyed.

Every year the parks services report hundreds of prosecutions and fines. Many other infringements are dealt with by a formal caution or just a friendly reminder – sometimes at the risk of abuse or violence. A Sydney Harbour ranger, patrolling by launch, spotted a beach party round an illicit fire. He went ashore to chide the group and was brutally bashed. Even organised crime impinges on parks: rangers in remote districts have had tense encounters with drug smugglers and marijuana growers.

Practical work to protect the environment is often sheer hard labour. Firebreaks and trails have to be maintained, and precautionary burns carried out. Most parks are at constant war with noxious weeds, feral animals or soil and sand dune erosion. Many have vandalism to contend with as well, or simply the inevitable wear and tear of heavy visiting. And parks services are increasingly taking over and trying to restore land damaged by other uses.

Rangers' reports form the basis of much of the park information that is distributed to the public. They also contribute to the resource studies and environmental impact assessments that precede major changes in management policies. Rangers may be called on for field observations to establish the numbers and movements of endangered animals, the location of rare plants, or the rate of decay of delicate landforms. Their judgments help decide where visitors are encouraged to go and what they are encouraged to do.

Educating the public is another big role. Some rangers spend much of their time running information and display centres or conducting guided walks. School parties receive special treatment, and rangers also go to schools for classroom talks. Landholders are offered advice on soil conservation, native tree care, wildlife protection, pest control and so on. Public relations addresses are often made to community groups – including some that are opposed to national parks. Hardest to win over are farmers who fear crop raids by animals from nearby parks, local body leaders who resent the loss of ratable land, and people whose livings depend on logging or mining.

Rangers of both sexes are highly trained in emergency procedures: fire fighting, search and rescue, first aid and sometimes flood response. Often they trap or kill animals – in the far north, their tasks may include buffalo musters and crocodile shoots. But little of a ranger's work is so exciting. Much more is mundane: fixing, cleaning and improving facilities, removing refuse, spraying weeds, supervising and informing visitors, issuing permits, collecting fees, answering mail and attending to clerical details.

Many ranger tasks are sheer drudgery: emptying garbage bins is not the worst of them

Carpentry skills ease a climb for nature trail parties

Winter duties in the Victorian Alps include clearing away snowdrifts so that skiers can get to their slopes – and then retrieving casualties

While tourists shun Kakadu's 'Wet', hard work goes on

THE POWER BEHIND THE PATCH

EMBLEMS patched on every park ranger's uniform are symbols of helpfulness and protection – and firm authority if it is needed. In enforcing certain laws on behalf of their state or territorial services, rangers have powers similar to those of the police. They carry identity cards stating their role as park wardens: their instructions must be obeyed.

Prosecutions for minor breaches of park rules are rare, but offenders who interfere with other people's enjoyment can be evicted. Formal letters of warning may be issued, so a ranger is entitled to ask for a culprit's name and address. To refuse is a further offence.

Under the laws that protect native plants and animals in parks, rangers acting on reasonable suspicion can search vehicles, containers and camps, seize any flora or fauna, and confiscate firearms and other hunting gear. In states where park rangers are also wildlife officers – not Victoria or Western Australia – their powers of search and seizure can extend to private property outside a park.

Positions are so sought after, however, that the parks services can be extremely selective. They usually insist on land management experience, and some states require applicants to hold a diploma in park management, environmental studies or natural sciences. And even that does not guarantee them a job – let alone any choice in where they work. Some busy parks employ a less formally qualified grade of 'park worker', chosen usually for manual skills. But the rangers themselves are expected to be competent and self-reliant in work such as carpentry and mechanical maintenance, along with bushcraft.

Staff with the highest qualifications usually work from regional centres or state head offices. They include architects, designers, lawyers, archeologists and publications specialists. But most are science graduates and technicians, conducting biological and environmental research. A few in each state concentrate on interpretation – the evaluation and explanation of park resources – and planning. This provides the main basis of management policy, which in turn determines how the rangers in the field have to do their work.

Queensland rangers collect data for turtle research

PARKS AND PEOPLE

Staying alive in the bush

FIRE IS BY FAR the greatest danger that visitors could face in national parks. When hot winds blow, bushfires can flare with little warning and approach with astonishing speed. But they move on just as quickly. Applying some commonsense safety procedures, no one need be killed or even badly burnt.

In the first place, parks consisting of eucalypt forests, dense scrub or heavily vegetated heathlands are best avoided when fire risks are extreme. They will be stiflingly hot and dusty anyway – hardly enjoyable unless they give access to rivers. Most parks display risk indicators near their entrances. And on the worst days, when total fire bans are declared, they are announced in all radio, newspaper and television weather reports. Check before setting out for a park; if there is a total ban in the district, consider changing your plans.

Fire bans are declared by statewide authorities. But park managements at any time can impose their own rules on the types of fires allowed. These are made clear on signs and in leaflets. Whichever sort of restriction applies, it is enforceable in court. Ignoring it could cost a stiff fine – even jail – or people's lives. For safety's sake alone the rules must be obeyed. And smokers have a particular responsibility to see that matches and butts are extinguished.

The killer in bushfires is not usually flame,

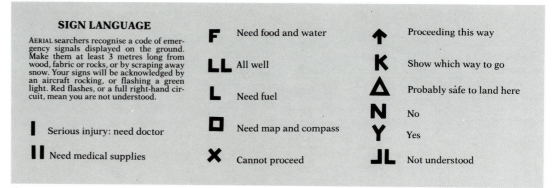

SIGN LANGUAGE

AERIAL searchers recognise a code of emergency signals displayed on the ground. Make them at least 3 metres long from wood, fabric or rocks, or by scraping away snow. Your signs will be acknowledged by an aircraft rocking, or flashing a green light. Red flashes, or a full right-hand circuit, mean you are not understood.

I Serious injury: need doctor
II Need medical supplies
F Need food and water
LL All well
L Need fuel
☐ Need map and compass
✗ Cannot proceed
↑ Proceeding this way
K Show which way to go
△ Probably safe to land here
N No
Y Yes
⌐⌐ Not understood

but radiated heat. Shield yourself from it. If you are on foot with a fire approaching, don't flee blindly. Look around for the best refuge – in a steep-banked creekbed, or behind a rock outcrop or a fallen log where the vegetation is thinnest. Keep low as you move – crawl if you must – to avoid smoke inhalation. If there is no shelter in sight, lie face down on a bare patch of ground. Scoop out a hollow for yourself if you can, and use loose soil to cover any exposed skin. When the main blaze has passed over you, move to where nothing is left to burn.

If you are in a car, stay there – it is your best possible shield against radiant heat. Cars are unlikely to catch fire, and sealed petrol tanks do not explode. Never try to drive through smoke. Park at the roadside – avoiding thick undergrowth and long grass – and turn on your headlights. Close windows and air vents, and block any chinks with paper or fabric. Get down on the floor and use the mats to cover exposed skin.

Bites and stings Never walk far into the bush without long trousers, socks and thick footwear. Take the greatest care where you tread on warm, sunny days, when snakes are most active. If you see a snake in your path, don't try to poke at it – annoyed in that way, it is most likely to strike. But if you stand well clear and make plenty of noise, it will go away.

Most of Australia's 140 snake species are venomous, but only about 15 are capable of killing humans. Unless you are expert in identifying species, however, regard any snakebite as dangerous. Apply a bandage that puts firm pressure *directly on the bitten area* – not a tourniquet. If a limb is bitten, immobilise it with a splint. Then quickly alert a ranger. The park may have its own venom-identification kit and anti-venom supplies.

A lethal species of funnel-web spider (*Atrax robustus*) is a threat to life only in the Sydney region. It is black and big – up to 7 cm across between leg-tips. Treat a funnel-web bite like a snakebite, with pressure bandaging and immobilisation. One other dangerous spider, the redback, may be found anywhere in Australia. Dark, with an orange-red stripe on its back, and measuring 2-3 cm across, its venom is slower-acting and bandaging is unnecessary if medical aid can be obtained quickly.

Bush ticks abound in eastern forests. Tiny when they attach themselves, they burrow into the skin and feed on blood for three or four days, swelling to about 1 cm across. Meanwhile they release a paralysing toxin that can lead to death, especially in children. If you have brushed through dense vegetation, inspect exposed areas of skin for the next three days – and have someone else examine your scalp. A lightly attached tick may be scraped off. One

Rangers and police practise rescue techniques in the Labyrinth at Cradle Mountain-Lake St Clair, Tas

BURNING WITH A PURPOSE

TASMANIAN rangers (pictured below) in Southwest National Park are lighting their own bushfire. It will turn hundreds of hectares into a blackened waste. But these men are making sure that a worse fire will not happen by accident.

The disaster potential of bushfires depends largely on how much fuel they can find. Preventive burning in national parks is ordered before the build-up of litter and undergrowth reaches a dangerous level. Not only the quantity of fuel but also its composition, distribution and moisture content are calculated – in some places with computers.

Frequent burning around the edges of parks is normally done by hand, but bigger tracts inside are more often fired with air-dropped incendiary capsules. Under most fire management programmes, only small sections of each park have to be burnt and closed off for regeneration. In the southeast, for example, preventive burning of as little as 5 per cent each year is enough to keep a whole area safe from full-scale destruction.

embedded more deeply can be killed with kerosene or turpentine, and perhaps prised out with tweezers. If this is not wholly successful, seek medical help. Leeches, which are bigger and less likely to escape notice in the first place, are seldom harmful. They drop out after about five minutes of feeding, or if killed with a burning cigarette end or twig. Don't pull them out – parts left in may cause an infection.

Big, aggressive saltwater crocodiles are increasing in some tropical parks. Remember, they are just as much at home in fresh water. Observe signs warning against swimming and take special care walking on riverbanks. If you find yourself near a basking crocodile, back off quietly. Never place yourself in its path to the water. It may use its tail to knock you out of the way – and one blow from a fullgrown 'saltie' could kill you.

Safety first Unless you are a fit and fully experienced bushwalker, stick to established paths and trails. Don't attempt a long journey through rugged or untracked country unless you have a party of at least three – then if someone is in trouble, another can stand by while the third goes for help. Always carry more water than you believe you will need, along with a first-aid kit and a compass, whistle, knife and waterproof matches. Don't start without obtaining up-to-date maps and telling a ranger of your intentions. And don't fail to report back when the trip is over, if you are asked to. Your negligence could spark a wasteful search operation.

If you are lost, assess your food and water supplies and ration them. Don't waste energy by moving about aimlessly. Seek shelter near an open space where signals can be seen from aircraft, and stay put. If you are forced to keep moving, leave messages along your route or mark it in some way, indicating your direction. To attract attention if other people seem to be nearby, give three whistles, shouts or mirror-flashes at regular intervals, and light a smoky fire of leaves or grass.

Fire-watching from the summit of Mt Lofty becomes a fulltime job during danger periods at Cleland Conservation Park, near Adelaide. Below: Backburning to contain a fast-moving wildfire

PARKS AND PEOPLE

How the public can help

IF YOU WOULD enjoy using some spare time to help maintain and improve a favourite national park, just ask. Almost certainly you will be put in touch with a band of volunteers already in action in the district. Most parks – especially those near major population centres – have arrangements with outside groups.

Hundreds of Australians find agreeable fresh-air exercise in voluntary park work at weekends and during holidays. There is room for more. Many tasks are menial: litter removal, weeding and tree planting are typical. But other jobs are highly constructive and add significantly to park amenities. Some are funded by community service clubs and business organisations.

Rapid volunteer response is credited with saving major parts of parks threatened by severe erosion after storm damage. Others, devastated by fire or flooding, have been brought back into public use surprisingly quickly thanks to donated labour. Sometimes a task is long overdue, but simply too hard for the park service to justify on a limited budget. 'Friends of the Prom', for example, trekked back and forth between Melbourne and Wilsons Promontory National Park to remove decades of painted graffiti from rocks at Refuge Cove.

Volunteers with manual trade skills, or experience in plant care on a large scale, are usually most welcome. Others who are adept at dealing with visitors, and can acquire the knowledge to interpret a park's natural features and answer questions, may be enlisted at busy times to help at information centres or take parties on guided walks.

Queensland volunteers pitch in to clear a trail

The Australian Trust for Conservation Volunteers, originating in Victoria but spreading nationwide in 1984, offers mobile squads of young people for national park assignments. These task forces usually camp on the site. Their first big accomplishment, in 1982, was the construction of 4.5 km of rabbit fencing at Hattah-Kulkyne National Park. Since then they have restored jetties, improved tracks, built footbridges and eradicated noxious weeds at various parks – and even cleaned up a disused guesthouse to accommodate visitors.

Members of the public are also entitled to have their say in the planning of national parks – where they should be and what activities should be allowed in them. Management plans are published, and in some states and the ACT the law demands that public comment be invited. Even without such a provision, there is nothing to stop an interested citizen making representations to the appropriate parks service or environment department. A sympathetic MP would probably give assistance.

But individuals have a hard time making themselves heard on national parks issues. Most arguments are too technical, resting on resource evaluations and environmental impact assessments. People seeking to sway government or park management decisions are advised to consult one of the National Parks Associations or a similar organisation.

ORGANISATIONS YOU CAN JOIN

PUBLIC organisations in every state and territory work for the establishment of new national parks, and generally to see that natural environments are not only conserved but also enjoyed.

National Parks Associations, which advance detailed cases to governments for the creation of new parks, are based in Sydney, Melbourne, Brisbane and Canberra. Equivalent bodies elsewhere are the SA Nature Conservation Society (Adelaide), the WA Conservation Council (Perth), the Tasmanian Conservation Trust (Hobart) and the NT Environment Council (Darwin).

National Parks and Wildlife Foundations, which conduct fund-raising appeals – such as NSW's annual 'Operation Noah' – to help acquire land for parks and conserve endangered animals, are based in Sydney and Adelaide. The **Australian Conservation Foundation,** with headquarters in Melbourne, focuses attention on wider environmental issues at a national level, but gives particular support to the national parks movement.

National Trusts, besides their work to save items of cultural heritage such as historic buildings, are active in promoting nature conservation. They have offices in all capital cities. The **Wilderness Society,** having triumphed in its No Dams campaign in Tasmania, has set up branches in nearly all mainland capitals.

World Wildlife Fund Australia, based in Sydney, raises money to preserve endangered species in Australia and some nearby Pacific islands. **Environment Centres** in all capitals and in many provincial cities provide public information and administrative facilities for the environmental movement as a whole. They can give you details of hundreds of other local and special-interest groups that may suit your purpose.

NOTE: Addresses at back of book

Outside helpers remove thorn apple, a noxious weed, from a creekbed in Snowy River National Park, Vic

Making the most of your visit

CREATION of a national park is no guarantee of stunning scenery or exciting activities. Australia's 500-odd parks are meant to preserve widely different environments. Not all may be to your liking. Many will lack the facilities to meet your particular needs. So in planning a visit, make sure you know what to expect.

From information in the regional guide sections that follow, readers can decide for themselves which parks are likely to hold most attraction and how much time they want to spend in them. Descriptions are down to earth – not glamorised. And the interest ratings are equally realistic. If a park rates low in 'day activities', for example, it means there is little to do but look around. There may not be enough to keep children amused for long.

In arranging a tourist itinerary, check on the availability of campsites. If you are interested in visiting several parks it may not be necessary to contact them all in advance – the capital city head office of the National Parks Service should be able to warn you of any difficulty. Queensland has a tourist pre-booking system, operated from Brisbane and regional offices, that covers all of its camping parks.

Consider the time of year and the weather, especially if a long journey outside your home district is involved. Most parks in the tropics, and many others inland, are far from enjoyable in summer. In the bushfire season, or if there have been heavy rains, call the enquiries number before setting out, to make sure that the park of your choice is open and accessible.

If you are travelling with a dog or cat, remember that you cannot take it into a national park. The menace that an escaped cat presents to wildlife is obvious. Few dogs are such efficient hunters – but their mere barking is enough to terrify native animals and disrupt their living patterns for days afterwards.

When you arrive at a park, or at a town office that looks after camping permits, pick up all the explanatory material offered. Anything that heightens your powers of observation will increase your enjoyment. And without full information, you may miss major points of interest. Nearly all parks have general maps. Some have leaflets to aid in bird spotting and plant identification, and special maps for bushwalks and self-guiding nature trails.

Public roads are kept to a minimum in all parks. Be prepared to leave your car in a designated parking area – never drive it into the bush – and see the sights on foot. It is by far the best way. Leaflets or signposts will tell you how long a walk should take, and whether it presents any difficulty.

Knowledge adds interest: an excellent example of park literature from the Northern Territory

WILDLIFE

The numbat, a rare termite eater, is protected at Dryandra Forest, WA

Scientists are intrigued by Eungella's gastric-brooding frog

Where animals

WERRIKIMBE National Park gained an extra 20 000 hectares of rainforest in 1984 – all for the sake of some mice. They are of a native species found in significant numbers only two years before. Now their home, on the upper Hastings River in northern NSW, should be secure.

Queensland has dedicated one of its national parks solely to preserve the habitat of an endangered species. The northern hairy-nosed wombat survives only at Epping Forest – formerly part of a cattle station on flat, semi-arid woodland west of Gladstone. Fencing keeps out grazing livestock and allows the regeneration of native grasses and scrub on which the wombat colony depends.

Successful husbandry of rare animals – especially those newly discovered – relies on complicated biological research and the scientific monitoring of populations and feeding habits. Only the national parks and wildlife services have the specialised resources for such work, so most conservation efforts are centred on their parks, or on some state parks under their management. Forestry and water catchment authorities play important co-operative roles.

A recent triumph of wildlife conservation has been the saving of the malleefowl in Victoria. It is the world's only mound-nesting bird living in arid regions. Clearing and grazing of its scrub habitats, along with bushfires, had all but wiped it out by the 1950s. But populations flourish

Parks were specially dedicated to rescue the endangered malleefowl. The male spends 8 months every year building a mound in which eggs are buried

Right: Only Kakadu, NT, has Leichhardt's grasshopper

For half a century the Hastings River mouse was known only from English museum specimens. Now it has a park section all to itself, where researchers are trying to discover its habits

find safety

Iron Range, Qld, is a haven for the golden-shouldered parrot

Left: A Queensland ranger examines a ghost bat – our only carnivorous species. Big colonies are seen at Fitzroy Caves and nearby Mt Etna

now in Little Desert, Hattah-Kulkyne and Wyperfeld National Parks. Mallee Cliffs National Park, in far western NSW, was established with the same aim.

Judging whether a species is truly rare can be difficult in Australia. Much of the fauna is small, secretive and nocturnal in habit. It is hard to find, let alone to count. And fires, floods and prolonged droughts lead to drastic fluctuations in numbers and distribution.

A highly unusual frog, discovered in 1972, disappeared after 1979. It lived in Kondalilla National Park and the neighbouring Conondale and Blackall Ranges of southeastern Queensland. Called the platypus frog because of its swimming action, it seemed to be the only frog in the world that never left water. And it was the world's only known gastric-brooding vertebrate. Females swallowed fertilised eggs and raised their young in their stomachs – somehow shutting off the production of digestive acids.

Rediscovery was hailed in 1983, when similar orange-coloured gastric-brooders were spotted far to the north in Finch Hatton Gorge, which leads out of Eungella National Park. But a captured specimen, compared with one of the Kondalilla frogs still alive in an Adelaide laboratory, proved to belong to yet another new species. The likelihood of other finds offers medical researchers high hopes of developing a drug to prevent human stomach ulcers.

The task of tallying animal populations is full of such surprises. Camping out in 1982 to count waterfowl, a wildlife officer in northwestern Tasmania made a convincing observation of a thylacine, or marsupial 'tiger'. Most people thought the species was extinct. But this animal's doglike head and black-striped, tawny back were unmistakable. Word of the sighting was withheld from the public for two years. If the breeding grounds of thylacines are traced, they will receive the strictest protection ever known.

Skunk-like in its markings, the striped possum of tropical rainforest parks is also remarkably smelly

RESTORATION

Nature gets another chance

WOUNDED LANDSCAPES are hard to heal. Even where full restoration is possible, the cost is often prohibitive. But national parks staff are succeeding, here and there, in turning back the clock. Their techniques were largely developed in old-established parks degraded by decades of heavy visiting. Now they are applied to recently resumed land that has suffered from other uses.

Most new inland parks have been at least partly grazed by livestock. The effect on natural vegetation is compounded by the persistence of feral animals – species that were introduced as domestic stock but now breed in the wild. Goats and pigs do the most widespread damage. Wild rabbits still bare the land in some districts, in spite of the sweeping eradication measures of the 1950s. High-country parks are often scarred by old logging trails or forestry roads, their margins invaded by exotic weeds. Steeper slopes may be subject to soil erosion.

When coastal parks are acquired, they frequently come with a legacy of dune erosion from off-road vehicles and ill-placed walking tracks. Many include old sand mining leases, or quarries where lime or building stone were extracted. Before the usual chores of removing noxious weeds and planting sand-binding grasses can start, the original land contours may have to be rebuilt.

Some park areas have a history of military use. They were taken over still bearing the marks of bombing or artillery practice and infantry exercises. Among the latest acquisitions are the various high headlands that make up most of Sydney Harbour National Park. These would not be available to the public now – suburban housing would have enveloped them – if they had not been reserved for 150 years or more as defence posts. Vantage points are capped with gun emplacements; the sandstone below is riddled with ammunition chambers, snipers' slits and connecting tunnels. The fortifications are worth keeping for their historical value – but their bare surroundings, stripped of soil by wind erosion, were an eyesore. Years of work and substantial funds are going into restoration

Sand mining roads scar a proposed park extension on Nth Stradbroke Island, Qld

Right: Regeneration of grazed land on Bogong High Plains, Vic, is a co-operative venture

A goat is fitted with a radio collar to track its movements

of the heaths and woodlands that greeted the First Fleet.

Bush regeneration calls for fine judgment, skilled work and inexhaustible patience. Attempts to make dramatic improvements overnight, simply by ripping out alien weeds or dumping new topsoil, are bound to fail. The same weeds – if not worse ones that are even faster-growing – will reappear, and probably work their way deeper into any natural bush nearby. Only a cautious approach, aimed at tipping the balance subtly towards native plants, is likely to succeed.

Managed regeneration of weed-infested bush starts from the least affected area and works towards the most degraded. In weeding, the soil is disturbed as little as possible and surface mulch is put back in place so that any native seeds lie at the proper level. The pace of progress is dictated by the capacity of seedlings to reclaim territory. They must have time to form a dense, diverse community in one zone – and planners must be convinced that it can be kept clear of weeds – before a neighbouring area is touched.

In rainforests the process is complicated by the interaction of plants. The different growth habits of weeds have to be considered, so that they are taken out in the correct order. If tall, leafy vines are removed first, for example, stronger light reaching the forest floor may spur the spread of ground creepers that choke off native seedling growth. Extensive regeneration projects, whether of rainforest trees or of eucalypts and their companions, take many years.

Control of feral animals calls for just as much patience. Little is achieved without a thorough knowledge of how they live in particular habitats. The breeding rate of a species may vary from place to place, depending mainly on climate and the availability of food. Patterns of movement also vary. Some plants and land are more easily damaged than others. All these factors influence a decision on how much control – which usually means killing – is necessary in a park, and what method will work best.

Wildlife suffers heavily from predation by feral cats and dogs and dingoes, and from the competition these and other species create for food, water and shelter. Rabbits and goats strip any vegetation they can reach

THE SCOURGE OF NATIVE WILDLIFE

CATS breeding in the wild are the most efficient of all predators. Their chief impact is on native birds, small mammals and reptiles. Indirectly they can also upset plant life, because they eat many of the animals that control insect pests.

Nearly all feral cats revert to a tabby appearance. Most are greyish, but on red outback soils more are ginger. In forested regions, where food is easily obtained, they are heavier than domestic cats but not noticeably bigger.

But in harsher country, it is survival of the fittest. The most powerful cats get the food – and the biggest toms take all the breeding opportunities. Supercats are evolving. Some stand twice as tall as their ancestors and are many times heavier. One giant shot in the Simpson Desert weighed 12 kg.

above ground, and pigs do even worse – they root into the soil with their snouts and leave it fit for nothing but weeds. Water buffalo in the Northern Territory trample and degrade wetlands that are important to tourism and vital to migratory waterfowl. And many feral species are potential carriers of exotic livestock diseases – tuberculosis and brucellosis, for example – that in uncontrolled conditions could be ruinous to the agricultural economy. In their extermination measures, parks services work in close co-operation with farming communities.

Feral pigs lay waste a waterhole at Kinchega, NSW

Trees return to former farmland at Organ Pipes, Vic

Heritage list

Mt Lidgbird on Lord Howe Island rises 777 metres from the edge of a coral-encrusted lagoon. The Lord Howe group, 700 km northeast of Sydney, is regarded as an outstanding example of an island system developed from submarine volcanic activity. Many of its plants and animals are found nowhere else. Much of the main island is protected under NSW national parks and wildlife laws as a 'permanent park'

Below: Forests crowd the deep gorge of the Franklin River in Wild Rivers National Park. This park forms the centre of the western Tasmanian World Heritage area, together with the neighbouring Southwest and Cradle Mountain-Lake St Clair National Parks

An obligation

NATURAL FEATURES of Australia figure importantly as World Heritage sites. Already listed are the Great Barrier Reef, Kakadu National Park, western Tasmania's chain of wilderness parks, the Willandra Lakes region of NSW, the Lord Howe Island group, and the rainforest parks and reserves of northern NSW. Uluru National Park, embracing Ayers Rock, is expected to be added.

Some great national parks overseas, such as Grand Canyon and Yellowstone in the USA, are among the nearly 200 other 'properties' on the list. But the majority are sites of ancient civilisations, or manmade structures of cultural importance. They include many famous cathedrals and palaces — along with the infamous Auschwitz concentration camp.

Inclusion of a natural area is a source of pride to any country. It confers recognition that the area is of world significance because it: represents a major stage of the

THE ANCIENT ROCK ART OF KAKADU

ABORIGINAL sites in Kakadu National Park, occupied for at least 25 000 years, include rock galleries of elaborate prehistoric paintings. Pictured are two from the hundreds seen by visitors to Ubirr (Obiri Rock).

Sand lunettes, windblown from the beds of the dried-up Willandra Lakes, hold evidence of human activity more than 30 000 years ago

to the world

earth's evolution; exemplifies continuing geological processes, biological evolution and human interaction with the environment; contains rare or superlative natural features or areas of exceptional beauty; or supports rare or endangered plants and animals.

But along with pride goes a heavy obligation. When a site is nominated for World Heritage listing, the nation responsible undertakes to ensure 'identification, protection, conservation, presentation and transmission to future generations ... to the utmost of its own resources'. The nominating nation is also obliged to obtain international assistance if it is needed to achieve those aims.

Some loss of sovereignty and secrecy is implied. That may be why the world list is noticeably incomplete: some countries refuse to compromise their privacy. In Australia's case the commitment made by the federal government clearly overrides states' rights. That was established in the High Court over the Tasmanian dam argument.

Australia's nominations are proposed by the Australian Heritage Commission. Its chairman and six members are part-timers appointed by the federal Environment Minister and drawn from a variety of professions in all states. They also supervise the selection and documentation of other important natural or cultural sites in Australia, and the compilation of a register of what is called the National Estate. Fraser Island, when it was rescued from sand mining, became the inaugural entry on that local list.

World Heritage nominations are received at UNESCO headquarters in Paris. Seventy countries have signed the convention that governs the listing procedure. Nominations go before a committee of 21 national representatives, with a membership that changes frequently so that every country gets a turn. The committee meets to approve listings towards the end of each year.

The Great Barrier Reef is the biggest Heritage area of all

PART THREE
A guide to the national parks of Western Australia and the Northern Territory

Parks are grouped on the basis of their accessibility from major population centres and their proximity to one another. In each region a pictorial selection is followed by a directory of parks. It gives their location, indicates their character and identifies the public facilities they offer. Comparative ratings, assessed by parks staff, are aimed at helping visitors decide on the destinations that will give them most satisfaction. As a further aid, the activities allowed in national parks are listed along with the parks in which they may be pursued.

Ayers Rock, Northern Territory

ESPERANCE & ALBANY REGIONS

The oldest land confronts the stormiest ocean

BOLD CONTRASTS await the traveller here. On one hand, jagged ranges overlook the coast and towering forests crowd sheltered inlets. On the other, windswept sandplains give a foretaste of the Nullarbor. Rainfall – nearly all of it during a chilly winter – declines from a liberal 1000 mm or more a year in the west to less than 300 mm in the east and north.

But the regions have their unities. Wildflowers, their species numbered in thousands, mount delightful spring displays in forest understoreys and on the most unpromising of heathlands. And everywhere the worn granite shield of the earliest Australia shows itself. It covers more than a third of the continent – but only here does it meet the sea.

Along most of the coast the shield forms low, tough headlands to take the brunt of boisterous Southern Ocean gales. Bays and landlocked havens strung between include King George Sound, the roomiest harbour in all Australia.

Dutch navigators, exploring this coast as early as 1627, kept cautiously out to sea after rounding Cape Leeuwin. They failed to spot the sound, or Esperance Bay, or any of the well-watered, wooded havens such as Nornalup Inlet. The best location found by Pieter Nuyts, the first explorer, was near Ceduna at the parched eastern end of the Bight. Even that was seriously proposed as the site of a Dutch colony, long before the British staked any claim on the continent. If Nuyts or the compatriots who followed him, such as Abel Tasman, had discovered just one of the better-favoured harbours to the west, the course of Nieuw Hollandt history might have been very different.

Rivers in these regions are the shortest-running in Australia, seldom originating more than 50 km from the coast. Those farthest east are seasonal trickles, most of them draining into saltmarshes before they can reach the ocean. Depressions in the hinterland plateau, marked on many maps as lakes, are salt pans that rarely receive water.

Tourist emphasis falls understandably on the coastal playgrounds, the forests of karri and other giant western eucalypts, and the rugged scenery of the Stirling and Porongurup Ranges. But the parks of the regions give an excellent sampling of a wide variety of other environments, including the semi-arid northern plains. Together they serve to protect many plants and animals that are found nowhere else in Australia.

Featured parks — Pages

1. Walpole-Nornalup 48-51
2. Stirling Range 52-55
3. Fitzgerald River 56-59
4. Cape Le Grand 60-61
5. Two Peoples Bay and Mt Manypeaks 62-65
6. Cape Arid 66-67

Your access and facilities guide to all national parks in these regions starts on page 68

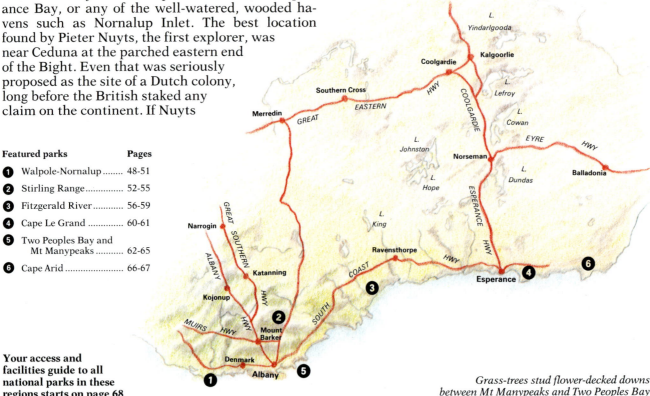

Grass-trees stud flower-decked downs between Mt Manypeaks and Two Peoples Bay

Dense heaths reach to the Southern Ocean shore at Long Point, which juts to the east of Mandalay Beach. It marks the limit of a lonely expanse called Nuyts Wilderness after Pieter Nuyts, the Dutch navigator who discovered this coast in 1627

Walpole-Nornalup National Park

Forests of karri and other giant eucalypts in the best-watered part of the southwest are preserved in 18 000 ha of splendid variety. A Southern Ocean coastline of 40 km includes granite headlands, wide beaches, dunefields, heath-clad slopes and tightly sheltered coves. Its central feature is the broad, landlocked basin of Nornalup Inlet. The Frankland and Deep Rivers feed into it from each side, winding out from between grandly wooded hills. Behind, invisible from the seaward side, a smaller basin formed by the Walpole River estuary is the site of the holiday township of Walpole.

Roads and walking tracks radiate from Walpole into the forests, where lookouts and riverside picnic spots are easily found. Other routes lead to the beaches, popular with fishing and boating enthusiasts as well as swimmers. Nuyts Wilderness, in the centre of the park between the Deep River and the sea, offers a rugged challenge to hikers seeking solitude.

Winds erode a coastal dune in spite of its flourishing vegetation. Some bare dunes are mobile

Karri forests overlook an arm of the Deep River and the tidal waters of Nornalup Inlet. Dunefields back the ocean coast beyond

Walpole-Nornalup National Park

Warren cedar overhang a flood-prone bend of the Deep River (left). Rainfall in the park and the catchments of its rivers averages more than 1000 mm a year. Karris (right), the mightiest trees of the west, flourish in the moist conditions and flowering shrubs grow profusely in the forest understoreys. But this region remains susceptible to fire: WA has no closed-canopy rainforest trees

Left: Granite boulders are strewn in the Frankland River

Above: Though badly burnt, this regenerating giant is identifiable as a red tingle – few eucalypts have this broadened, buttressed base

STIRLING RANGE NATIONAL PARK

Exposed for eons and deeply weathered, the Stirling Range originated as a submarine sedimentary bed laid down about 2500 million years ago, then intensely folded and thrust up from the south. Its upper layers are of quartzite and sandstone, overlying shales and slates, while the low plain surrounding the range is formed of even older granite

In all of Western Australia, this is the only place where a flurry of snow may be seen. Conical peaks, bluffs, rock chimneys and saddles rise with unlikely abruptness along an east-west line of 55 km, from a farming plain only 200 metres above sea level. A dozen summits top 750 metres, with Bluff Knoll in the east supreme at 1073 metres. A park of 115 000 ha embraces the entire range.

Seasonal creeks cut into gullies and flats between the peaks, supporting small stands of jarrah, marri and wandoo eucalypt forest. But the Stirlings are better known for the diversity and floral brilliance of their shrubs and heath plants. Many are unique, having evolved in isolation when most of the region lay under the sea. Some snails, trapdoor spiders and frogs also show localised variations. Birds, insects and reptiles abound. Marsupials range from the big western grey kangaroo to the thimble-sized honey possum.

Walkers are in their element here. Those venturing far should notify the ranger, be prepared for extremes in temperature, and carry water.

52 ESPERANCE AND ALBANY REGIONS

Showy shrubs cloak the lower slopes of Toolbrunup Peak (1052 metres). A summit track takes 2 hours from a foothills car park

Eucalypt woodlands are carpeted with low shrubs and heaths. More than 800 flowering species are found in the park – some of them unique, and confined to certain peaks in the range

Blue-flowering Stirling Range smokebush

Pink mountain bell – unique

Paper-heath – found in the far south

STIRLING RANGE NATIONAL PARK

Kingia – 'black gin' – grass-trees grow to 5 metres

Hovea is a woody shrub of the pea family

Dryandra is peculiar to Western Australia

Rose coneflower – common on heathlands

Mountain pea grows nowhere else

Salty flats surround the upper reaches of Hamersley Inlet, which is usually flushed out by river waters in winter. To the west, quartzite peaks of the Mid Mt Barren group slope steeply to a lonely coast

Fitzgerald River National Park

Intermittent streams flowing from the Barren Ranges feed sand-barred inlets along a 100 km coastline between the fishing settlements of Bremer Bay and Hopetoun. East of the Fitzgerald River, which cuts across the centre of the 329 000 ha park, the flanks of Mid Mt Barren (457 metres) and other peaks drop directly to the Southern Ocean, forming sea cliffs or steep scree slopes. But most of the coast has beaches of dazzling quartz sands, backed by dunes and sandplains. Inland the Fitzgerald and Hamersley Rivers have cut narrow gorges with tall, colourful cliffs. Their valleys and some other watercourses have woodlands of mallee eucalypt, melaleuca and a eucalypt called swamp yate. On the sandy heathlands, mallee scrub has a dense and diverse understorey of flowering shrubs.

Access within the park is very limited. Four-wheel-drive tracks may be closed in wet months to control the spread of dieback disease.

Right: Dense heaths stabilise dunes beside Fitzgerald Inlet, which is usually cut off from the ocean by a sand bar

Left: Binding grasses protect Fitzgerald Beach from wind erosion. Rip currents are frequent along this coast – would-be swimmers should seek a ranger's advice on the safer sections, and never venture far out. Rock anglers must be wary of freakish 'king' waves

Hibiscus withstands exposure on windy coastal sites

Fitzgerald River National Park

Leaves of royal hakea last for up to five years, their colour steadily growing richer

Lambertia attracts butterflies

WA has its own tea-tree species

Heathland shrubs grow in an almost bewildering profusion among mallee eucalypts (left and below). Fitzgerald River was the first area in WA to be internationally listed as a biosphere reserve. It is managed so that its plant and animal communities serve as a model against which changes in similar areas can be judged

Blossom of the bell-fruited mallee, a heathland eucalypt

Southern plains banksia

A weathered granite tor stands sentinel over Thistle Cove, where waves of the Southern Ocean swing in (right) to create fine conditions for swimming and rock fishing

CAPE LE GRAND NATIONAL PARK

Purple enamel orchid, one of a ground-growing group found only in the southwest

Humped outcrops of bare granite and gneiss mark the eastern limits of Esperance Bay. Coves indenting the headland are the most popular destinations in a 31 000 ha park. Agreeable beaches allow safe swimming, fishing and boating. Short scenic walks can be taken through richly flowering sandplain heaths to hilly mallee scrublands commanding good views of the coast and the Recherche Archipelago. Birds abound and native bees nest in the shelter of rock caves and overhangs. Energetic visitors can tackle a 15 km, full-day trail linking the coves between Le Grand Beach and Rossiter Bay. The western half, skirting Mt Le Grand (345 metres) to Hell Fire Bay and Thistle Cove, is hard going and requires experience.

Silver tea-tree – recently rediscovered after a century

Frenchman Peak (262 metres) is easily climbed by a track up the eastern flank

White spider orchid

Downy stackhousia

Tumbled sandstone boulders frame the mouth of the Waychinicup River, which flows out at Hassell Beach, to the east of Mt Manypeaks

Two Peoples Bay and Mt Manypeaks

Efforts to preserve the rare, noisy scrub bird have focused attention on two areas of outstanding scenic merit. **Two Peoples Bay Nature Reserve** was created on Mt Gardner headland and its hinterland after the bird was rediscovered there in 1961. Part of its 4750 ha to the north and east of Mt Gardner is closed to the public and vehicles must stay on formed gravel roads. Not far east, between Normans Beach and the Waychinicup River, **Mount Manypeaks Nature Reserve** provides a second home for the scrub bird colonies. There are no tracks in the 1300 ha park, and Mt Manypeaks is closed to walkers. The nature reserve now lies within **Waychinicup National Park**, established in 1991.

Oxylobium blooms among tors of granite. Smooth outcrops of the ancient rock occur strikingly (below) on colourful heathlands overlooking Two Peoples Bay

Scarlet banksia is common on sandy soils

Curry flower is named for its scent

Leschenaultia

Southern cross, a perennial herb

Prickly bitter pea

Bald Island is a sanctuary for the quokka, a short-tailed wallaby. Uncommon on the mainland, its only other stronghold is Rottnest Island, not far from Perth.

Two Peoples Bay and Mt Manypeaks

Cape Arid National Park

Beaches of Yokinup Bay make a sandy sweep of 20 km from the mouth of the Thomas River to a granite headland capped by Mt Arid (356 metres). An hour's climb from a coastal track, the peak gives superb views of a complex shoreline and dozens of islets of the eastern Recherche Archipelago. Easier vantage points are gained near the rivermouth camping ground at Belinup Hill, which has a self-guiding nature-circuit of 1 km. Behind dunes and swampy clay flats, this area is well vegetated with colourful heath plants and banksia, acacia and mallee eucalypt scrub. Inland, the 280 000 ha park consists mostly of sandplains. But in the north it is dominated by the wooded Russell Range, where razorback Mt Ragged rises to 585 metres.

Mt Ragged, standing out on the distant skyline, can be reached along a four-wheel-drive road. Fingers of granite shelter shallow, sandy bays (right) where swimming and fishing are popular

PARKS OF THE ESPERANCE & ALBANY REGIONS

FACILITIES
- Cabins
- Caravan park
- Equipped picnic area
- Bush camping allowed
- Lavatory building
- Established campsite
- Campsite but no car access

Note: Popular parks without campsites usually have public camping grounds nearby. If in doubt, call enquiries number.

PARK RATINGS: No interest ✘ Some interest ✔ Major interest ✔✔ Outstanding ✔✔✔

1. Boorabbin National Park
465 km NW of Esperance. Goldfields weather district. Park stretches 28 km along the Great Eastern Highway, 5 km on either side, between Southern Cross and Coolgardie.

A narrow roadside park of 26 000 ha in rolling country protects tracts of sandplain heath. In spring, the low shrubs and smaller plants present a dazzling spectacle of colour and variety.
BEST TIME: Spring.
TEL: (08) 9021 2677.
FAX: (08) 9021 7831.
ADDRESS: PO Box 10173, Kalgoorlie 6430.

Scenic enjoyment ✔
Day activities ✘
Family camping ✘
Hard bushwalking ✘

2. Cape Arid National Park
125 km E of Esperance. Eucla weather district. Car access from Fisheries Road E of Esperance to main camping area. 2WD access half way into park, 4WD needed after that.
DESCRIPTION: Page 66.
NOTES: Campers must take water. Pack campers are advised to inform ranger of intentions – much of the park is waterless.
WARNING: Swimmers need advice on safe beaches.
BEST TIME: Spring for wildflowers, summer for water sports.
TEL: (08) 9071 3733.
FAX: (08) 9071 3657.
ADDRESS: As for Eucla.

Scenic enjoyment ✔✔✔
Day activities ✔✔✔
Family camping ✔✔✔
Hard bushwalking ✔✔

3. Cape Le Grand National Park
50 km SE of Esperance. Southern Coastal weather district. Car access from Merivale Road or Fisheries Road. Within the park, most roads are now bituminised – only some 10 km of road have a good gravel surface.
DESCRIPTION: Page 60.
NOTES: Pack campers are advised to notify ranger at park entrance. All campers should take gas stoves. Fee charged at established camping areas at Lucky Bay and Le Grand Beach.
BEST TIME: Spring, summer.
TEL: (08) 9071 3733.
ADDRESS AND FAX: As for Eucla.

Scenic enjoyment ✔✔✔
Day activities ✔✔✔
Family camping ✔✔✔
Walking, climbing ✔✔✔

4. Eucla National Park
930 km E of Esperance. Eucla weather district. Eyre Highway passes park near WA/SA border.

Literal high point of the park is Wilson Bluff, reached from the highway by a gravel track. It gives impressive views of the sheer sea cliffs of the Great Australian Bight. Mallee scrub and heaths cover most of the 3340 ha park. Nearby, the abandoned Eucla telegraph station, dating from the construction of the original transcontinental telegraph line, is part-buried among encroaching sand dunes.
BEST TIME: Spring.
TEL: (08) 9071 3733.
ADDRESS AND FAX: PO Box 234, Esperance 6450.

Scenic enjoyment ✔✔
Day activities ✔
Family camping ✘
Hard bushwalking ✘

5. Fitzgerald River National Park
185 km NE of Albany, 250 km W of Esperance. Southern Coastal weather district. Car access to eastern side of park is from Ravensthorpe–Hopetoun road or from West River road off South Coast Highway. Roads are partly gravel; 4WD to Quoin Head when wet. Access to western end is via Devils Creek Road or Jacup Road South. Fair gravel roads; 4WD to Fitzgerald Inlet.
DESCRIPTION: Page 56.
NOTES: No drinking water in the park. Pack campers should report to ranger before starting walk. Fees charged at established camp areas, in addition to park fees.
WARNINGS: Swimmers need advice about safe areas. 'King' waves may endanger anglers. Shale cliff edges may be unstable.
BEST TIME: Spring, summer.
TEL: (08) 9842 4500.
FAX: (08) 9841 7105.
ADDRESS: 120 Albany Highway, Albany 6330.

Scenic enjoyment ✔✔✔
Day activities ✔✔
Family camping ✔
Hard bushwalking ✔✔

6. Frank Hann National Park
230 km NW of Esperance. Goldfields weather district. Car access through park by Norseman–Lake King road (gravel – part rough).

A park of nearly 61 500 ha straddles the road for a stretch of 55 km. It provides a variety of habitats from sand heaths to mallee scrub and eucalypt woodlands – surprising in an area of low rainfall. Among flowers in spring, the red rapier feather flower is particularly striking.
WARNING: Area remote and waterless – travellers must be equipped for outback survival.
BEST TIME: Spring.
TEL: (08) 9071 3773.
ADDRESS AND FAX: As for Eucla.

Scenic enjoyment ✔
Day activities ✘
Family camping ✘
Hard bushwalking ✘

7. Goongarrie National Park
515 km N of Esperance, 100 km N of Kalgoorlie. Goldfields weather district. Car access from Kalgoorlie to Menzies highway (sealed road).

Mulga, at the southern edge of its range, meets mallee scrub and York gum woodlands in a park of 60 356 ha. Emu bush and acacias are prominent shrubs over a ground cover of speargrass. Wildflowers bloom as ephemerals if soaking rain falls.
WARNING: Area remote dry – visitors must be fully equipped for outback travel.
BEST TIME: Winter and spring, after good rains.
TEL: (08) 9021 2677.
ADDRESS AND FAX: As for Boorabbin.

Scenic enjoyment ✔
Day activities ✘
Family camping ✘
Hard bushwalking ✘

8. Hassell National Park
50 km NE of Albany. Southern Coastal weather district. Car access through park on South Coast Highway between Albany and Bremer Bay.

A roadside reserve, merely some 150 m wide, extends for 34 km. Its 1265 ha are dense with wildflowers in spring. Among birds in the tall shrubs are red wattlebirds and New Holland, white-necked and singing honeyeaters.
NOTE: No drinking water.
WARNING: Snakes are common.
BEST TIME: Spring.
TEL AND ADDRESS: As for Fitzgerald River.

Scenic enjoyment ✔
Day activities ✘
Family camping ✘
Hard bushwalking ✘

① Boorabbin NP
② Cape Arid NP
③ Cape Le Grand NP
④ Eucla NP
⑤ Fitzgerald River NP
⑥ Frank Hann NP
⑦ Goongarrie NP
⑧ Hassell NP
⑨ Mount Frankland NP
⑩ Peak Charles NP
⑪ Porongurup NP
⑫ Stirling Range NP
⑬ Stokes NP
⑭ Torndirrup NP
⑮ Two Peoples Bay Nature Reserve
⑯ Walpole-Nornalup NP
⑰ Waychinicup NP
⑱ West Cape Howe NP
⑲ William Bay NP

PARKS OF THE ESPERANCE & ALBANY REGIONS

9. Mount Frankland National Park
120 km W of Albany. Southern Coastal weather district. Car access via Weld or Beardmore roads off Southwestern Highway, or Thompson road from Walpole on South Coast Highway.

Mt Frankland itself is a large granite dome rising 100 m above the surrounding plains of karri and tingle trees. A 2 km walk from the base to the summit provides spectacular views to the coast. The 30 830 ha park has a variety of vegetation: tall karri forest near the Deep River in the west; in the east, the Frankland River, surrounded by jarrah woodland and swampy flats skirts the Soho Hills where the spectacular red-flowering gum occurs naturally.
BEST TIME: Spring, summer.
TEL: (08) 9840 1207.
FAX: (08) 9840 1251.
ADDRESS: South Western Highway, Walpole 6398

Scenic enjoyment ✓✓✓
Day activities ✓✓
Family camping ✗
Hard bushwalking ✓✓

10. Peak Charles National Park
185 km N of Esperance, 100 km SW of Norseman. Goldfields weather district. Car access from Kumari on Coolgardie–Esperance Highway by good gravel road to base of Peak Charles.

Two granite outcrops, Peak Charles and Peak Eleanora, dominate mallee-covered sandplains, eucalypt woodlands and vast salt lakes in the 40 000 ha park. Precipitous cliffs of Peak Charles (651 m) are broken into numerous boulder-strewn shelves with curved gorges. Nesting into the walls of the peak are small meadows where several varieties of orchid and unusual species of darwinia are found.

Only experienced bushwalkers should make the one-hour climb to the top of Peak Charles. A trail ends halfway up, then scrambling up steep sections is necessary.
NOTES: Camping allowed only at the foot of Peak Charles.
BEST TIME: Spring, autumn.
TEL: (08) 9071 3733.
ADDRESS: As for Eucla.

Scenic enjoyment ✓✓
Day activities ✓
Family camping ✗
Hard bushwalking ✓✓

11. Porongurup National Park
50 km N of Albany, 20 km E of Mount Barker. Southern Coastal weather district. Car access from Porongurup township; from Woodlands Road off Mount Barker to Porongurup Road; or from Millinup Road off Chester Pass Road from Albany.

High rainfall attracted by the Porongurup Range, 12 km long and up to 670 m high, enables karri forest – once widespread in the area – to survive on the higher slopes. Below the giant trees flourish native wisteria, water bush, hazel trees and blue-flowered hovea trees. Farther down, jarrah and marri grow above meadows of wildflowers.

In this park of 2572 ha, western grey kangaroos are common. Wedge-tailed eagles hover overhead, using up-draughts from the peaks, and scarlet and yellow robins, western rosellas, white-tailed black cockatoos and tree martins are plentiful. Rufous tree-creepers are cheeky foragers of crumbs around picnickers, and the karri trees in flower attract flocks of purple-crowned lorikeets, heard but seldom clearly seen. A scenic drive gives views of the distant Stirling Range, and four walking tracks lead to peaks, past sculptured rocks and a huge balancing boulder.
NOTE: Walkers should take care of slippery rocks. No camping in park. Entrance fee.
WARNING: Snakes are common in summer.
BEST TIME: Year-round.
TEL: (08) 9842 4500.
ADDRESS AND FAX: As for Fitzgerald River.

Scenic enjoyment ✓✓
Day activities ✓✓
Family camping ✗
Walking, climbing ✓✓

12. Stirling Range National Park
80 km N of Albury. Great Southern and Southern Coastal weather districts. Chester Pass Road from Albany (sealed) crosses park. Most roads within park are unsealed.
DESCRIPTION: Page 52.
NOTES: Bush campers and rock climbers should sign books and pay fee at registration posts near Bluff Knoll turnoff or at park headquarters. Fee charged at established camping area.
VISITOR CENTRE: At Moingup Spring near Toolbrunup turn-off. Additional information centre at Bluff Knoll turn-off.
BEST TIME: August to November.
TEL: (08) 9842 4500.
ADDRESS AND FAX: As for Fitzgerald River.

Scenic enjoyment ✓✓✓
Day activities ✓✓✓
Family camping ✓✓✓
Walking, climbing ✓✓✓

13. Stokes National Park
86 km W of Esperance. Southern Coastal weather district. Car access via good gravel road from South Coast Highway.

Encompasses 10 700 ha surrounding Stokes Inlet and features long beaches and rocky headlands backed by sand dunes and low hills. The tranquil waters of the inlet provide opportunities for fishing, boating, canoeing and windsurfing, but not sailing as there are extensive areas of shallows and rocks. A 1 km circuitous walking trail runs along the escarpment overlooking the inlet. The inlet and associated wetlands support a rich variety of wildlife, which is especially popular with birdwatchers.
NOTES: Take water and gas stove. Self-registration entry fee.
BEST TIME: Spring, summer.
TEL: (08) 9071 3733.
ADDRESS AND FAX: As for Eucla.

Scenic enjoyment ✓✓✓
Day activities ✓✓
Family camping ✓✓
Hard bushwalking ✓

14. Torndirrup National Park
15 km S of Albany. Southern Coastal weather district. Car access via Frenchman Bay Road.

Chasms, cliffs, blowholes and beaches between rugged headlands rim a 3940 ha park reaching east to Flinders Peninsula, the southern flank of King George Sound. Heavy seas funnelling up a crevice in the granite occasionally drench visitors on a viewing platform 25 m above the sea at the Gap. Sealed roads lead to other vantage points. Shelving slopes of rock tempt fishermen, but 'king' waves have caused several drownings.

Experienced and energetic walkers can make their way along a poorly defined track through prickly parrot bush to Bald Head, the most easterly point of the promontory. The return trip of 6 hours gives the visitor views of the ocean, the islands in the sound, and Albany, 10 km to the north. What early explorers took to be dead coral in the sand on top of Bald Head are calcified roots of shrubs. Among the birds in the stunted coastal scrub which includes a local bottlebrush with deep red flowers, New Holland honeyeaters are abundant.
BEST TIME: Spring.
TEL: (08) 9842 4500.
ADDRESS AND FAX: As for Fitzgerald River.

Scenic enjoyment ✓✓✓
Day activities ✓
Family camping ✗
Hard bushwalking ✓

15. Two Peoples Bay Nature Reserve
40 km E of Albany. Southern Coastal weather district. Car access to picnic area along Two Peoples Bay Road from Lower King. Access to one part of the reserve is entirely prohibited.
DESCRIPTION: Page 62.
NOTES: Walkers attempting Mt Gardner or Cape Vancouver trails are advised to notify reserve officer. No fires or pets allowed.
WARNING: Beware of snakes.
VISITOR CENTRE: At car park.
BEST TIME: August to January.
TEL: (08) 9842 4500.
ADDRESS AND FAX: As for Fitzgerald River.

Scenic enjoyment ✓✓
Day activities ✓✓
Family camping ✗
Hard bushwalking ✓✓

16. Walpole-Nornalup National Park
120 km W of Albany. Southwest weather district. Car access from Walpole, or from Peaceful Bay Road off South Coast Highway at Bow Bridge.
DESCRIPTION: Page 48.
NOTE: Fee charged at established camping areas.
BEST TIME: Year-round (spring for flowers and whales).
TEL: (08) 9840 1207.
FAX: (08) 9840 1251.
ADDRESS: South Western Highway, Walpole 6398

Scenic enjoyment ✓✓✓
Day activities ✓✓✓
Family camping ✓✓✓
Hard bushwalking ✓

17. Waychinicup National Park
50 km E of Albany. Southern Coastal weather district. Access from Hassell Highway 11 km beyond Manypeaks township to Cheyne Beach road then via rough gravel track.

The outstanding coastal scenery and magnificent floral displays in spring are two of the principal visitor attractions of this 3982 ha national park, established in 1991. Fishermen find the tranquil waters of the Waychinicup River enticing. There is a camping ground at nearby Cheyne Beach. **Mount Manypeaks Nature Reserve** lies within the park, strictly as an ecological reserve. (**DESCRIPTION:** Page 158).
NOTE: Campers must pay a fee. Free gas BBQ; wood fires are not allowed.
BEST TIME: Spring (for wild flowers) and summer.
TEL: (08) 9842 4500.
ADDRESS AND FAX: As for Fitzgerald River.

Scenic enjoyment ✓✓✓
Day activities ✓
Family camping ✓
Hard bushwalking ✗

18. West Cape Howe National Park
30 km W of Albany. Southern Coastal weather district. Car access from Lower Denmark Road and Hortons South Road (good gravel). All other access 4WD only (lower tyre pressure for driving on sand). The main features of this 3500 ha park are Shelley Beach, Torbay Head, West Cape Howe and Bornholm Salmon Holes beach. The coastline is backed by coastal heathland and swamps with a small area of karri forest near the main park entrance on Torbay Hill.

Popular with fishermen, hang gliders, naturalists and rock climbers. Camping fee at established camp area (Shelley Beach) with free gas BBQ.
WARNING: Beware of dangerous waves.
BEST TIME: Spring, summer.
TEL: (08) 9842 4500.
ADDRESS AND FAX: As for Fitzgerald River.

Scenic enjoyment ✓✓
Day activities ✓
Family camping ✓
Walking, climbing ✓✓

19. William Bay National Park
70 km W of Albany. Southwest weather district. Car access from South Coast Highway 14 km W of Denmark. Bus services pass park.

The narrow sandy beaches and low headlands of the 1740 ha park produce many pleasant fishing spots and the protected waters of Greens Pool make it popular for swimming. Between the dunes grow thickets of stunted Western Australian peppermint, and away from the coastal there is a small track of karri forest. To the west Parry Inlet provides a breeding ground for waterfowl.
BEST TIME: Spring, summer.
TEL: (08) 9840 1207.
FAX: (08) 9840 1251.
ADDRESS: South Western Highway, Walpole 6398

Scenic enjoyment ✓
Day activities ✓
Family camping ✗
Hard bushwalking ✓

PERTH REGION
Stubborn forests under an alien threat

FORESTS OF the Darling Scarp, giving a priceless margin of greenery to the cleared and developed Swan coastal plain, are dominated by stately jarrah. Reaching 60 metres in height, in defiance of fire, drought and infertile soils, *Eucalyptus marginata* is the west's great survivor. Its timber has long been prized for quality furniture and termite-resistant construction, and jarrah forests were heavily cut over early in the state's history. But for half a century, along with its companion plants in a unique forest community, it has been under threat from an introduced disease.

A microscopic, soil-borne fungus invades the feeder roots and hinders their taking up moisture and nutrients. Called *Phytophthera cinnamomi* or cinnamon fungus, it is thought to have originated in tropical Southeast Asia. In eastern Australia the disease does its most serious damage to mangroves. In the west hundreds of plant species are susceptible – grass-trees, cycads, banksias, dryandras, casuarinas and so on.

Many plants, especially the banksias, are killed quickly. But jarrah in most conditions can fight the fungus for years. Infected trees succumb gradually, losing their outermost leaves in a process called 'dieback'. Between 1940 and 1965, thousands of hectares of forest were wiped out. The disease can also have a dire effect on banksia woodlands and heathlands, notably along the south coast.

For a time, the death of all jarrah forests and many other plant communities seemed inevitable. The west faced scenic deprivation, loss of a valuable timber resource and a dramatic loss of wildlife habitats. In recent years, however, the rate of spread of the disease has declined markedly and the outlook is more hopeful. Armed with improved scientific knowledge of the conditions that favour the fungus, park and forest managers have been able to apply effective quarantine measures.

Spores of the fungus are spread most easily when soil is shifted – often accidentally on vehicle tyres. Park visitors are urged to keep to formed, well-drained roads and to heed any closure signs.

In spite of the presence of dieback the jarrah forest is readily accessible and offers a wide variety of activities in the autumn, winter and spring months – picnicking, bush walking, canoeing and camping. For the more adventurous there is perhaps the most satisfying long-distance forest walk in Australia. The Bibbulmun Track starts at Kalamunda at the scarp edge near Perth and links parks and forests along a route of more than 400 kilometres south to Shannon Park, in the karri forest near Manjimup.

Featured parks	Pages
❶ John Forrest	72-73
❷ Walyunga	74-75
❸ Leeuwin-Naturaliste	76-79
❹ Pemberton	80-81
❺ D'Entrecasteaux	82-83
❻ Nambung	84-85
❼ Kalbarri	86-89
❽ Kalamunda	90

Your access and facilities guide to all national parks in this region starts on page 91

Sandstone grandeur in Murchison Gorge. Kalbarri National Park

John Forrest National Park

A number of good walktrails throughout the park lead over rocky hills, through eucalypt woodlands to quiet pools and tumbling rapids and waterfalls along Jane Brook. Flanked by suburbia, John Forrest lies between Great Eastern Highway and Toodyay Road. The park is busiest in spring, when wildflowers and birdlife combine with bushland scenery to attract visitors. Western Australia's first national park, it was proclaimed in 1900, when it was called Greenmount; it was renamed later after the distinguished explorer and statesman Lord Forrest. The main picnic area of rock-walled gardens, walkways and steps was developed during the Depression years of the 1930s by sustenance workers. The park covers some 3000 ha, providing a good representation of Darling Scarp vegetation; high vantage points give good views of the Swan coastal plain.

One-sided bottlebrush (calothamnus) is endemic to Western Australia

Right: Paperbarks shade a peaceful stream. Many of the park's waterways have swimming holes, and Jane Brook is dammed to make a big pool near picnic grounds and restaurants

Wandoo dominates a rocky woodland slope

Open woodlands spread along the seaward side of the Darling Scarp. Grass trees surround a granite outcrop

Grey cottonhead, a small herb

Flowing briskly after its plunge over the Darling Scarp, the Swan River starts its journey through Perth to Fremantle

Left: A once-majestic red gum (marri) which has been seriously affected by drought

Walyunga National Park

Perched on the steepest slopes of the Darling Scarp, a wooded park of just under 1800 ha drops from 280 to 30 metres above sea level. It is deeply cut by the valley of the Swan River, which levels out to form spacious pools in a smooth granite bed – popular for swimming and boating. When the river runs high after winter rains, canoeists test their skills in rapids upstream of Wooroloo Brook and Long Pool.

Aborigines used a well-drained, sandy area close to Walyunga Pool as a seasonal encampment – the biggest found in the Perth district. Erosion of the topsoil after a pioneer ploughing attempt has revealed hundreds of stone and bone tools and hunting weapons.

Walking trails lead from riverside picnic areas into eucalypt woodlands dominated by jarrah on leached upland soils, marri on better ground and wandoo on the valley slopes. Well-watered shrubs around granite outcrops flower magnificently in late winter and spring.

Sugarloaf Rock, a deeply weathered granite mound near Cape Naturaliste, is the southernmost breeding site of the red-tailed tropic bird

Wind erosion of dunes behind Quarry Bay, just north of Cape Leeuwin, bares remnants of a limestone bed

Clematis and hardenbergia

Native violet (Hybanthus calycinus)

Leeuwin-Naturaliste National Park

Between the two horn-like capes that jut from the south-western corner of the continent, ancient granites and gneisses are capped by an 80 km ridge of limestone. Nowhere is the Indian Ocean coastline more varied than here, at its beginnings. Wide beaches and dunefields are interspersed with rocky headlands and sections of high, windswept cliffs. Nearshore islets and reefs strewn along most of the coast add to its scenic diversity. Inland, water permeating the limestone has hollowed out caves of high scientific importance and tourist interest.

The former Cape Leeuwin and Cape Naturaliste National Parks and some linking areas acquired in the 1970s are amalgamated in a park of 15 500 ha occupying most of the coast; the only major break is in the middle around the Margaret River. Vegetation ranges from wind-stunted heaths and mallee scrubs to eucalypt forests, including tall stands of jarrah in the south.

Leeuwin-Naturaliste National Park

Crystalline formations are seen in a remarkable variety of shapes at Yallingup Cave, 40 metres below the ground. They are caused when rainwater, containing carbonic acid from the air and decayed plant matter, percolates down and dissolves limestone. The slight evaporation of clinging droplets leaves a gradually growing residue, shaped according to the way the liquid flows or splashes. Colour variations result from the presence of traces of other minerals, such as iron

Pemberton National Parks

Rufous tree-creeper

Reserves clustered around the forestry township of Pemberton protect hilly stands of wet eucalyptus forest – mainly karri but including jarrah and marri – with lush understoreys of spring-flowering shrubs. The principal national parks are Beedelup (1500 ha), Warren (1400 ha) and the much smaller Gloucester (48 ha).

Of the rivers that flow through the parks, the Beedelup has cascades with a total fall of more than 100 metres, and the Warren offers good swimming and trout fishing. Gloucester has the highest fire lookout tree in the world, over 60 metres high. Scenic roads and walking trails criss-cross the district.

Left: Wattles and lomandras surround a cascade of the Beedelup Falls, crossed above and below on a circuit walk

Herbs and flowering shrubs form a continuous understorey for tall jarrah, mixed with karri and marri in Warren National Park. Tan wattle (left) and white clematis and hardenbergia (above) are prominent here

Huge limestone boulders have tumbled into the sea at remote Point d'Entrecasteaux

Left: 'Lamb's poison', a common heathland pea, bears a single flower on each of its stems

Limestone cliffs are dissolving at Point D'Entrecasteaux, halfway along the coastal stretch of the park.

D'Entrecasteaux National Park

Beaches and cliffs reaching for 130 km from Black Point near Augusta to Long Point west of Walpole are backed by high sand dunes, built and pushed inland by the persistent westerly currents and winds of the Southern Ocean. Six major streams and rivers, including the Warren and Shannon, drain through the park and empty into its coastal waters. They create a belt of swamps and lakes that separates the coast from forested hills and farming country.

The park extends inland between 5 and 20 km, covering an area of 118 000 ha. Behind varied coastal forms of limestone and granite – relieved by cliffs of volcanic basalt at Black Point – the plant and animal communities of the dunes, wetlands and woodlands remain little disturbed or studied, and may hold surprises. Jarrah, bullich, yate and peppermint trees form low woodlands in places where the prevailing southerly sea wind is reduced or blocked, with scattered pockets of karri.

Paperbarks are swamped in the sand-barred waters of Broke Inlet, a waterfowl haven near Walpole

Nambung National Park

Scaevola: salt-resistant

Spikes and knobs of limestone – many taller than a house, others no bigger than pencils – stud the sands of the Pinnacles Desert. They are the main inland feature of an undeveloped park of 17 500 ha occupying dunefields and sandplains just south of Cervantes township. Other interest in the park is directed towards its 26 km coastline, where sandy beaches are accessible on foot or by four-wheel-drive. Swimming is safe in reef-protected waters and the area has a good reputation for fishing. But the roads can be rough and sometimes sand-drifted. Travellers whose main concern is to see the Pinnacles may prefer to take a bus tour from Cervantes.

The Nambung River makes a chain of waterholes through part of the park before disappearing into a cave system – inaccessible to the public. Woodlands flourish nearby, but visitors see mostly low scrubs and heaths, flowering colourfully in late winter and spring.

Nambung's pinnacles began to form centuries ago when lime-rich sands, blown inland, created high mobile dunes. Rain leached the lime from their upper layers cementing the lower sand into a soft limestone. Stabilising plants spread an acidic layer of soil and humus over the dunes, accelerating the leaching. A hard topping of calcrete formed over the limestone (seen today as a cap on many pinnacles). Plant roots exploited cracks in the calcrete; water seeped down the channels, continuing the subsurface erosion of the limestone. The pinnacles, remnants of that limestone layer, were exposed as the prevailing wind blew away the surrounding quartz sand

An unsealed road takes visitors to a lookout above the Pinnacles Desert, then loops through it for a closer inspection

Nature's Window, carved by windblown sand, frames a view of Murchison Gorge from a lookout at The Loop

KALBARRI NATIONAL PARK

Extraordinary river gorge scenery is matched in grandeur by soaring sea cliffs in a vast sandplain park of 186 000 ha. Heath wildflowers and acacia scrublands, at their best in late winter and spring, complete a visual feast.

Until about 2 million years ago the Murchison River wandered to the coast across a flat bed of sandstone. Then as earth movements forced an uplift of the rock, the river continued its course by cutting deeper and deeper. Its old meanders remain, so the gorge of more than 80 km is unusually twisted and looped. Unsealed roads lead to a succession of exceptional vantage points over multi-hued sandstone walls and side gorges, falling as much as 150 metres to the waterway and its avenue of river red gums.

On the coast south of Kalbarri township the same ancient sandstone is overlain by younger sedimentary strata and capped by limestone. Cliffs and steep gullies show an even greater range of colour than is seen upriver, and a striking variety of layered erosion patterns.

Swimming and fishing are possible on the coast but seas are treacherous. Pools in the gorge are safe unless the river is in flood. Short walks can be taken; longer hiking or canoeing require permission in writing.

Pink pokers grevillea

White-flowered grevillea

Diplolaena

Guinea flower

Right: *Hawk's Head overhangs the twisting Murchison River*

Kalbarri National Park

Coastal sandstones weathered by spray (above) and wave action (below) show thin lenses of harder iron deposits

Right: From smashed or ground-down boulders, plucked from cliffs above, the ocean reclaims what it created 400-500 million years ago

Deep gullies dissect Kalbarri's forbidding sea cliffs. It was here that the Dutch navigator Francis Pelsaert set adrift two mutineers in 1629. If they got ashore and managed to survive, those men were the first known European residents of Australia

Pimelea, a riceflower, favours sandy slopes

Kalamunda National Park

Piesse Brook trickles through a hilly little park on the high slopes of the Darling Scarp. Eucalypt woodlands are carpeted with heath plants, blossoming profusely in late winter and spring. The 375 ha park, managed primarily as a plant reserve in an area of spreading suburban development, has no public facilities. But trails connect to make pleasant walks of up to 4 hours. Hikers can cool off in Rocky Pool waterhole if the brook is running.

Watsonia, a South African plant of the iris family, invades the margins of Piesse Brook

Right: Flowering spikes of the common grass-tree attract honeyeaters and bees

PARKS OF THE PERTH REGION

1. Alexander Morrison NP
2. Avon Valley NP
3. Badgingarra NP
4. Christmas Island NP
5. D'Entrecasteaux NP
6. Drovers Cave NP
7. Gooseberry Hill NP
8. Greenmount NP
9. John Forrest NP
10. Kalamunda NP
11. Kalbarri NP
12. Leeuwin-Naturaliste NP
13. Lesmurdie Falls NP
14. Moore River NP
15. Mount Lesueur NP
16. Nambung NP
17. Neerabup NP
18. Pemberton's NPs
19. Scott NP
20. Serpentine NP
21. Shannon NP
22. Tathra NP
23. Tuart NP
24. Walyunga NP
25. Watheroo NP
26. Yalgorup NP
27. Yanchep NP

FACILITIES

- Cabins
- Caravan park
- Equipped picnic area
- Bush camping allowed
- Lavatory building
- Established campsite
- Campsite but no car access

Note: Popular parks without campsites usually have public camping grounds nearby. If in doubt, call enquiries number.

PARK RATINGS: No interest ✗ Some interest ✓ Major interest ✓✓ Outstanding ✓✓✓

1. Alexander Morrison National Park

270 km N. Central West weather district. Car access from Brand Highway 45 km N of Badgingarra, on Coorow road (gravel).

Late-blooming wildflowers flourish on sandplain heathlands covering most of the 8500 ha park, which straddles a little-used road between Coorow and the coast. Birds are abundant on the heaths and in a few areas of low eucalypt woodland and mallee scrub.

NOTE: No water supplies.
BEST TIME: Early summer.
TEL: (02) 9652 7043.
ADDRESS: PO Box 62, Cervantes 6511.

Scenic enjoyment ✓✓
Day activities ✗
Family camping ✗
Hard bushwalking ✗

2. Avon Valley National Park

80 km NE. Lower West weather district. Car access off Toodyay Road via Morangup and Quarry Roads (gravel for 12 km).

Bald Hill commands impressive views of the Avon River beginning its descent of the broken Darling Scarp. Emu Spring Brook, a tributary, spills in a 30 m waterfall after winter rains. Jarrah, wandoo and marri dominate dry eucalypt forest in a hilly park of nearly 4400 ha, with western Christmas trees and grass-trees prominent in the understorey.

Graded maintenance tracks aid bushwalking. One follows the river downstream, allowing an interesting overnight hike past the Avon's junction with the Brockman River – the two become the Swan – and down into Walyunga National Park. The river is easily crossed in summer and autumn. But the terrain is steep and rocky; sturdy, rubber-soled footwear is needed.

NOTE: Self-registration and payment of an entry fee are mandatory. Water at picnic sites.
BEST TIME: Autumn, winter, spring.
TEL: (08) 9574 2540.
ADDRESS: PO Box 881, Toodyay 6566.

Scenic enjoyment ✓✓
Day activities ✓✓
Family camping ✓
Hard bushwalking ✓✓

3. Badgingarra National Park

205 km N. Central West weather district. Car access by Brand Highway (skirts park).

Spring-flowering heaths deck 13 100 ha of gently rolling, sandy country, relieved in places by banksia woodlands. The park is principally a reserve for the rare black kangaroo paw, but its plant communities include many colourful dryandras, hakeas and grevilleas. Some are relics of a wetter climate, having affinities with plants now more common in the southwest.

A 2 km wildflower walk identifies important species. Elsewhere, fire trails lead around and across the park. There are no other tracks, but walking is relatively easy.

NOTES: Take water. Fires prohibited.
BEST TIME: August–September.
TEL: (08)96 52 7043.
ADDRESS: As for Alexander Morrison.

Scenic enjoyment ✓
Day activities ✓
Family camping ✗
Hard bushwalking ✗

4. Christmas Island National Park

2620 km NW. Air access by government charter flights weekly from Perth – enquiries (08) 9481 1705 or by private charter from Perth – enquiries (8) 9481 1200.

Christmas Island is situated south of Java at roughly the same latitude as Darwin. Until recently the principal industry on the island was phosphate mining, but the emphasis now is towards tourism. The National Park covers 8720 ha or approximately two-thirds of Christmas Island as well as most of its fringing reef. Included within the park is much of the island's remaining rainforest as well as the habitat of the endemic and endangered Abbott's Booby seabird. In addition to its extensive seabird rookeries, the area is renowned for its land crabs: the world's largest remaining

PARKS OF THE PERTH REGION

population of coconut, or robber, crabs is on the island and, during the early wet season, the migration of 130 million red crabs to the sea is a spectacular sight. Permanent streams in the Dales area of the park provide habitats for the protected blue crab as well as unusual vegetation assemblages. Walking trails and 4WD and 2WD tracks provide access throughout the park. A picnic site and raised boardwalk have been constructed in the Dales area.
BEST TIME: Dry season for fishing, wet season for crabs.
TEL: (08) 9164 8382.
FAX: (08) 9164 8080.
ADDRESS: PO Box 63, Christmas Island, Indian Ocean, WA 6798.

Scenic enjoyment ✔✔✔
Day activities ✔✔
Family camping ✔
Hard bushwalking ✔

5. D'Entrecasteaux National Park
350 km S. Southwest weather district. Access: turn-off on South Western Highway to Mandalay Beach 12 km W of Walpole or into Broke Inlet road 3 km N of Burnett at eastern end; Windy Harbour road 8 km S of Northcliffe at centre. Other access tracks are suitable for 4WD only.
DESCRIPTION: Page 83.
BEST TIME: Year-round (spring for wildflowers).
TEL: (08) 9776 7095 (eastern end), (08) 9776 1207 (western end).
ADDRESS: As for Pemberton's.

Scenic enjoyment ✔✔✔
Day activities ✔
Family camping ✔
Hard bushwalking ✔✔✔

6. Drovers Cave National Park
250 km N, near Jurien Bay. Central West weather district. 4WD access off Brand Highway–Jurien road.

Caves containing limestone drip formations and important deposits of prehistoric mammal bones are the focus of a park occupying nearly 2700 ha of dry sandplain heathlands and banksia woodlands. It is not developed for general visiting and Drovers Cave itself is kept locked. Experienced cavers may inspect some others by arrangement with the ranger in charge at Nambung.
NOTES: Take water. Fires prohibited.
BEST TIME: Spring.
TEL: (08) 9652 7043.
ADDRESS: As for Nambung.

Scenic enjoyment ✔
Day activities ✘
Family camping ✘
Hard bushwalking ✘

7. Gooseberry Hill National Park
20 km E. Lower West weather district. Car access off Lascelles Parade via Williams Street, Gooseberry Hill.

A steep 30 ha patch of wandoo, jarrah and marri woodland high on the Darling Scarp is known in adjoining suburbs as the Zigzag. Embankments and cuttings of a disused switchback railway carry a sightseeing road that descends from a popular lookout. Wildflowers are prolific in spring.
BEST TIME: August–September.
TEL: (08) 9298 8344.
ADDRESS: As for John Forrest.

Scenic enjoyment ✔✔
Day activities ✔
Family camping ✘
Hard bushwalking ✘

8. Greenmount National Park
25 km E. Lower West weather district. Car access off Great Eastern Highway at Greenmount, via Darlington and Padbury Road. Buses along highway.

Dry eucalypt woodlands occupy 58 ha of a spur of the Darling Scarp, overlooking the Helena Valley and giving good views of Perth. Spring wildflowers attract many visitors.
NOTE: Fires prohibited.
BEST TIME: August–September.
TEL: (08) 9298 8344.
ADDRESS: As for John Forrest.

Scenic enjoyment ✔✔
Day activities ✔
Family camping ✘
Hard bushwalking ✘

9. John Forrest National Park
25 km E. Lower West weather district. Park adjoins Great Eastern Highway between Greenmount and Glen Forrest. Car access at three points on highway (vehicle entrance fee). Foot access also from Swan View or Hovea. Buses along highway.
DESCRIPTION: Page 72.
NOTE: Permit needed for bush camping.
BEST TIME: Winter and spring (August – October for flowers).
TEL: (08) 9298 8344.
FAX: (08) 9298 9426.
ADDRESS: c/o PO, Glen Forrest 6071.

Scenic enjoyment ✔✔
Day activities ✔✔✔
Family camping ✘
Hard bushwalking ✔✔

10. Kalamunda National Park
25 km E. Lower West weather district. Car access via Kalamunda to Spring Road and Schipp Road.
DESCRIPTION: Page 90.
BEST TIME: Winter and spring. (July–October for flowers).
TEL: (08) 9298 8344.
FAX: (08) 9298 9426.
ADDRESS: As for John Forrest.

Scenic enjoyment ✔✔
Day activities ✔
Family camping ✘
Hard bushwalking ✔

11. Kalbarri National Park
550 km N, 170 km N of Geraldton. Central West weather district. Car access from North West Coastal Highway by Ajana–Kalbarri road (traverses park). Vehicle entrance fee. Flights Perth–Geraldton–Kalbarri most days. Buses Perth–Kalbarri some days. Bus tours of park from Kalbarri daily (weather permitting).
DESCRIPTION: Page 86.
NOTES: Accommodation of all kinds available nearby in Kalbarri. Overnight hikers must have written permission from NP office – only groups of five or more considered safe in remote areas. No water except from river. No camping in park.
WARNING: Hiking in remoter parts should not be attempted in summer heat.
BEST TIME: Winter and spring.
TEL: (08) 9937 1140.
FAX: (08) 9937 1437.
ADDRESS: Box 37, Kalbarri 6536.

Scenic enjoyment ✔✔✔
Day activities ✔✔
Family camping ✘
Hard bushwalking ✔✔✔

12. Leeuwin-Naturaliste National Park
265–350 km S. Southwest weather district. Car access from many points along Caves Road.
DESCRIPTION: Page 77.
WARNING: Crumbling cliff edges are dangerous.
BEST TIME: Spring to autumn.
TEL: (08) 9752 1677.
FAX: (08) 9752 1432.
ADDRESS: 14 Queen Street, Busselton 6280.

Scenic enjoyment ✔✔✔
Day activities ✔✔
Family camping ✘
Hard bushwalking ✔

13. Lesmurdie Falls National Park
25 km E. Lower West weather district. Car access through Forrestfield or Lesmurdie. Bus along Lesmurdie Road.

Among 56 ha of the dry eucalypt woodlands characteristic of the Darling Scarp, Lesmurdie Creek cascades into a pool surrounded by broad slabs of granite. New trails offer fine views of the park. The western trail follows the creek through the park while the eastern trail leads to a vantage point giving a view of the falls and Perth.
BEST TIME: Winter and spring.
TEL: (08) 9298 8344.

ADDRESS: As for John Forrest.
Scenic enjoyment ✔✔
Day activities ✔✔
Family camping ✘
Hard bushwalking ✘

14. Moore River National Park
120 km N. Lower West weather district. Brand Highway passes park.

Rose banksia has its only habitat in this undeveloped park of 17 500 ha, among low woodlands of other banksias, pricklybark and western Christmas tree. Other notable spring-blooming wildflowers are black and golden kangaroo paws and verticordia. The park is a good example of the sandy heathlands of the northern coastal plains, including some dry dune systems and seasonal and permanent swamps. Walkers can take advantage of an extensive network of fire trails.
NOTE: Dry, remote area. All water must be carried in. Camping not permitted.
BEST TIME: Spring.
TEL: (08) 9561 1004.
ADDRESS: As for Yanchep.

Scenic enjoyment ✔✔
Day activities ✘
Family camping ✘
Hard bushwalking ✘

15. Mount Lesueur National Park
250 km N. Central West weather district. Access by 4WD off Brand Highway–Green Head road.

The rugged terrain and the abundance of poisonous plants in this relatively recently established (1991) national park has spared it from agricultural clearing. Extensive coal deposits are found and where the coal reaches the surface is the greatest diversity of plants – mostly shrubby species less than 1 m tall, which contributes to the country's uninterrupted vistas. Mt Lesueur itself is the area's highest feature, and to the west lie sand dunes, swamps and low limestone ridges. During the winter months, gold and purple sun orchids, Cleopatra's needles, can be found scattered over the rocky summit of Mt Lesueur. Queen of Sheba orchids and bronze orchids are also found in the area. Other attractive plants include black kangaroo paw, honeybush and staghorn bush, while plants that have survived from ancient times include the kingia, Lesueur hakea, cork mallee and trumpets. The fauna is rich in birds (particularly heath-dwelling species) frogs and reptiles. Some 15 native mammals, including four species of dunnarts, have been recorded in the area.
BEST TIME: Year-round.

TEL: (08) 9652 7043
ADDRESS: PO Box 62, Cervantes 6511.

Scenic enjoyment ✔✔
Day activities ✘
Family camping ✘
Hard bushwalking ✘

16. Nambung National Park
245 km N. Central West weather district. Car access by Brand Highway, turning off for Cervantes. The road into the park (partly gravel) starts 2 km from Cervantes.
DESCRIPTION: Page 84.
NOTES: Fires prohibited. Camping and caravan facilities and other accommodation available at Cervantes.
BEST TIME: Spring.
TEL: (08) 9652 7043.
FAX: (08) 9652 7340.
ADDRESS: PO Box 62, Cervantes 6511.

Scenic enjoyment ✔✔✔
Day activities ✔✔✔
Family camping ✘
Hard bushwalking ✔

17. Neerabup National Park
30 km N. Lower West weather district. Park adjoins Wanneroo Road, car access by Quinns Rocks road, bisecting park. Foot access to southernmost area from Burns Beach road.

Between Lake Joondalup and Carabooda Lake, a narrow strip of nearly 1100 ha gives an unusually varied representation of coastal sandplain country. In the south the park is wooded with jarrah, casuarina and banksia. In the southeastern corner the limestones of old dune systems outcrop, supporting a dense heath of parrot bush. To the north, woodlands are dominated by massive tuarts with an understorey of heath plants or banksias. Brilliant displays of wildflowers are seen from July to November.

The park has no facilities for visitors but walkers can use fire breaks; also the Yaberoo–Budjera Heritage Trail crosses the park, giving a wonderful opportunity for walkers to witness the wildflower display when in season. The length of the park can be covered in a day.
BEST TIME: July to November.
TEL: (08) 9561 1004.
ADDRESS: As for Yanchep.
Scenic enjoyment ✔
Day activities ✔
Family camping ✘
Hard bushwalking ✔

PARKS OF THE PERTH REGION

18. Pemberton's National Parks (Beedelup, Gloucester, Warren)
340 km S. Southwest weather district. Car access to main parks from Pemberton via Vasse Highway and via Northcliffe road for Gloucester. Foot access on Bibbulmun Track.
DESCRIPTION: Page 80.
NOTE: Main public facilities are in Warren National Park. Fee charged for Warren River campsites.
BEST TIME: Spring and autumn.
TEL: (08) 9776 1207.
FAX: (08) 9776 1410.
ADDRESS: Kennedy Street, PO Box 20 Pemberton 6260.

Scenic enjoyment ✓✓✓
Day activities ✓✓✓
Family camping ✓✓
Hard bushwalking ✓✓

19. Scott National Park
330 km S. Southwest weather district. 2WD access off Brockman Highway E of Alexandra Bridge. Boat access from Augusta or Alexandra Bridge.

A park of nearly 3300 ha protects wetlands and wooded slopes on the east bank of the Blackwood River above its junction with the Scott River, and straddles the Scott for about 3 km upstream. Jarrah, marri and karri are prominent in the woodlands, which have a dense understorey of flowering shrubs. Swamps provide widespread breeding habitats for waterfowl.

The area is largely undeveloped and difficult to reach except by boat. It is most often seen, unknowingly, by tourists taking scenic launch cruises up the Blackwood River from Augusta.
BEST TIME: Spring to autumn.
TEL: (08) 9752 1677.
FAX: (08) 9752 1432.
ADDRESS: As for Leeuwin-Naturaliste.

Scenic enjoyment ✓✓
Day activities ✓
Family camping ✗
Hard bushwalking ✓

20. Serpentine National Park
60 km S. Lower West weather district. Car access off Western Highway South by Falls Road. Vehicle entrance fee. Gates closed 1800–0800 (check on entry).

Dry eucalypt forests, dominated by jarrah and marri, are preserved in a hilly park of 4362 ha. The area has drawn picnic parties since before World War I, when the government was urged to appoint a caretaker to defend it from 'trainloads of excursionists' every wildflower season. The chief attractions originally were the Serpentine Falls and a big granite pool below, where the Serpentine River descends the Darling Scarp. Although the river was dammed upstream in the 1950s to augment Perth's domestic water supplies, the falls can generally be seen throughout the year, drying up only in the driest of seasons. Swimming is not encouraged as the water is untreated.

The geographically restricted Darling Range ghost gum, *Eucalyptus laelie*, may be seen on the walk to the falls. Wildflowers are prolific in season (August–October), over 300 species occuring within the park. The management tracks within the park provide good access to all areas; the terrain is challenging and care must be exercised. Excellent picnic areas, including barbecue facilities, are available, visited by free-ranging western grey kangaroos.
BEST TIME: Spring and autumn – very hot in summer.
TEL: (08) 9525 2128.
ADDRESS: Falls Road, Serpentine 6205.

Scenic enjoyment ✓✓✓
Day activities ✓✓✓
Family camping ✗
Hard bushwalking ✓

21. Shannon National Park
360 km S. Southwest weather district. South Western Highway Manjimup–Walpole traverses parks, gravel roads lead off. Foot access on Bibbulmun Track.

Covering 53 500 ha and the entire basin of the Shannon River, the park contains a great range of forest scenery and many different wildlife habitats. It embraces the Shannon River, from its headwaters north of the highway to its mouth at Broke Inlet. During the dry season the water level sinks, and the river retreats to a series of pools in a dry bed.

Hilly forests in the north and centre of the park are dominated by karri, or mixtures of karri, jarrah and marri, usually with dense understoreys of karri wattle. Towards the south, jarrah woodlands and banksias occur at the margins of seasonally flooded flats supporting sedges and herbs.

Camping and day-visit facilities have been developed near the highway at the old Shannon townsite. Easy trails include a self-guiding interpretative walk and a special route for disabled people. Gravel roads of varying quality – some 4WD only – lead to most parts of the park and fire breaks aid bushwalking. The river is suitable for swimming at many points; it can be negotiated by canoe for 5–10 km upstream from Broke Inlet.
BEST TIME: March to May or September to January.
TEL: (08) 9776 1207.
FAX: (08) 9776 1410.
ADDRESS: As for Pemberton's.

Scenic enjoyment ✓✓
Day activities ✓✓
Family camping ✓✓
Hard bushwalking ✓✓

22. Tathra National Park
300 km N. Central West weather district. Car access from Brand Highway by Eneabba–Carnamah road (traverses park – last section unsealed).

Surrounded by agricultural land, Tathra has been left undeveloped as a reserve for the wildflowers of its rolling sandplain heathlands and banksia woodlands. Diverse plant communities in the 4322 ha park include unique species of dryandra and daviesia.
NOTE: Only day visiting permitted.
BEST TIME: Spring.
TEL: (08) 9652 7043.
ADDRESS: As for Alexander Morrison.

Scenic enjoyment ✓
Day activities ✗
Family camping ✗
Hard bushwalking ✗

23. Tuart National Park
203 km S. Southwest weather district. Access on Bussell Highway 15 km NE of Busselton, between Capel and Sabina River.

The 2500 ha national park protects the largest remaining pure forest of tuart, a slow-growing hardwood unique to the southwest of Western Australia. Before European settlement the understorey of the forest is thought to have been clear of the peppermint that now dominates it as a direct result of grazing and frequent fires.

The park forms a conservation area that supports a wide variety of birds and animals, and is the preferred habitat of the rare and endangered western ringtail possum. The estuaries of the Ludlow, Abba and Sabina rivers are wetlands of international significance, and are the breeding grounds for 80 species of water birds. The nearby restored Wonnerup House, built in 1859, gives a glimpse of life in the pioneer era.
BEST TIME: Spring for wildflowers, late summer for birds.
TEL: (08) 9752 1677.
ADDRESS: 14 Queen Street, Busselton 6280.

Scenic enjoyment ✓
Day activities ✓
Family camping ✗
Hard bushwalking ✓

24. Walyunga National Park
40 km NE. Lower West weather district. Car access off Great Northern Highway, turning E 8 km past Upper Swan. Vehicle entrance fee.
DESCRIPTION: Page 75.
NOTE: Camping by arrangement with the ranger.
BEST TIME: April–November.
TEL: (08) 9571 1371.
ADDRESS: PO Box 54, Bullsbrook 6084.

Scenic enjoyment ✓✓
Day activities ✓✓✓
Family camping ✗
Hard bushwalking ✓

25. Watheroo National Park
220 km N. Central West weather district. Car access through southern sections of park off Midlands Road by Watheroo–Badgingarra road (gravel).

Heathlands in a basin of quartz sands occupy most of an undeveloped park of 44 500 ha. Wildflowers include some rare species, and others that are usually associated with the southwest rather than the dry midlands plains. Small areas are covered by eucalypt woodlands or tall banksia scrub.
NOTE: No water in park. Bush camping may be permitted after consultation with ranger.
BEST TIME: Spring.
TEL: (08) 9652 7043.
ADDRESS: As for Alexander Morrison.

Scenic enjoyment ✓
Day activities ✗
Family camping ✗
Hard bushwalking ✗

26. Yalgorup National Park
120 km S. Lower West weather district. Car access from Old Coast Road S of Mandurah, turning off for Preston Beach. Buses along Old Coast Road.

Lakes and swamps form a chain between parallel lines of dunes and old limestone ridges, providing breeding habitats and feeding grounds for thousands of waterfowl. More than 100 species have been seen in the 13 150 ha park. Its eucalypt woodlands include tuart, jarrah and marri with banksias, peppermint and casuarina below. Some exposed slopes have coastal heath communities dominated by acacias, dryandras, hakeas and grass-trees.

Short walking trails skirt some of the lakes. Fire breaks aid cross-country walking, but the ranger should be notified beforehand. The park coastline has excellent beaches.
BEST TIME: Winter and spring for wildflowers; summer for birdwatching and beach pastimes.
TEL: (08) 9582 9333.
FAX: (08) 9582 9725.
ADDRESS: PO Box 1266, Mandurah 6210.

Scenic enjoyment ✓✓
Day activities ✓✓
Family camping ✓
Hard bushwalking ✓

27. Yanchep National Park
55 km N. Lower West weather district. Car access by Wanneroo Road (traverses park). Vehicle entry fee to lake and caves area. Perth–Two Rocks bus service.

Big grey kangaroos come out at sundown to graze a golfcourse and sports oval. The scene neatly captures the contradictions of Yanchep, which was intensively developed as a recreational park before it came under national parks management. Much of it was landscaped, and the swampy margins of Yanchep Lake were drained and reclaimed as lawns around what became Loch McNess. Private companies operate a shop and a licensed inn. Koalas, imported from across the continent, are kept in enclosures by the lake and examples of western wildflower species are displayed in planted beds.

Yanchep does have more natural areas, wooded with marri, jarrah and tuart or banksias and casuarinas, with flowering heaths and grass-trees in the understorey. Numerous fire breaks can be used for up to a day's bushwalking far from the sight or sound of the busy lake area. To the east the 2800 ha park has limestone caves with interesting drip formations. Visitors may take part in guided tours of Crystal Cave; an entry fee is charged.
NOTE: No camping.
BEST TIME: Spring.
TEL: (08) 9561 1004.
FAX: (08) 9561 2316.
ADDRESS: Yanchep NP, Yanchep 6035.

Scenic enjoyment ✓
Day activities ✓✓✓
Family camping ✗
Hard bushwalking ✓

Mammals and reptiles of Western Australia

Western Australia is the ancestral land; its landforms are older than elsewhere on the continent. Separated from the east by vast and inhospitable distances and itself divided north from south by desert, the state has ancient plants and rare and unique animals. Among the animals are the scaly-tailed possum, found only in the northwest Kimberley, the quokka and, today, the numbat. This anteater once lived across South Australia and into western New South Wales but now exists only in pockets in the Stirling Range and Dryandra Forest. As well, distinct western subspecies and geographical races of animals have emerged – as has happened with the black-footed rock-wallaby

Scaly-tailed possum – only member of its genus

Quokka – once common in the damp southwest, its largest population is now on arid Rottnest Island

Black-footed rock-wallaby – one of a small population at Cape Range

Western grey kangaroo – a protected species

Shingle-back lizard – short-legged and slow-moving, it relies on a fierce display to deter intruders

Numbat – predation and burning of habitat have drastically reduced its numbers

Olive python – found in the rocky hills of the northwest

Bungarra lizard – local name for Varanus gouldii, sometimes also known as the racehorse goanna

Australian sea lions – at Cape Le Grand

Carnarvon & Port Hedland Regions

Miners spur interest in a long-neglected land

PURISTS in conservation may shudder at the very idea of iron-ore mining leases in Karijini National Park, and of surveyors and prospectors roaming in the other parks and reserves of the northwest. The fact is that the miners had prior claims in this harsh, arid corner. Their activites have brought it back to life.

Without the roads, airstrips and water bores built by mining companies and the local knowledge they accumulated, it is doubtful whether ecologists could have gained enough appreciation of the area to judge what was most worth conserving. Certainly, from a public point of view, the unusual natural features of the northwest would have remained unreachable and largely unknown. Touring is a practical proposition only because of the improved communications and other amenities that came with a huge investment in mineral extraction, processing and export facilities.

Oddly enough, this was the very first part of Australia to be frequented by Europeans. Dirk Hartog commanded the first authenticated landing in 1616, near Carnarvon, and his fellow-Dutchmen came to know the northwest coast well in the following decades. John Brooks, an Englishman, navigated North West Cape waters as early as 1622. William Dampier explored ashore in 1688 and 1699 – first as a pirate, then as a Royal Navy captain.

Every adventurer noted tides of phenomenal range and frightening power. Inland they saw a parched, hostile environment holding no prospect of trade or treasure. Ill-starred attempts in the 1860s to grow cotton and raise beef cattle reinforced that view. Even the frantic military efforts of World War II brought few lasting changes.

The transformation started with oil. Australia's first commercial field was discovered in 1952 at Rough Range, close to what is now Cape Range National Park. This park's only formed roads were built for exploratory surveys; its Shothole Canyon car park was a drilling platform. Nearby Exmouth emerged as the first of the northwestern boomtowns, soon to be eclipsed by port after port to the east. Though their impetus comes from continued development in petroleum and iron ore exploitation, they have become tourist destinations in their own right.

A less publicised industry, salt production, commands attention at both Carnarvon and Port Hedland. Vast evaporation beds, marked by dazzling white storage mounds, are the most efficient on earth. They take advantage of a hot and extraordinarily cloudless climate. The sun beats down for well over 3500 hours in some years. Drenching summer monsoons of the 'Top End' do not reach this northwest corner: its usually meagre rainfalls show slight peaks in both winter and summer. Prolonged heavy rains are rare. Perhaps that is fortunate – they come only with violent tropical cyclones.

Your access and facilities guide to all national parks in these regions is on page 105

Featured parks	Pages
❶ Cape Range	98-99
❷ Karijini	100-103
❸ Millstream-Chichester	104

Shales and conglomerates of Dales Gorge, in Kirijini National Park, were laid down 2000 million years ago

Sheltered by a distant reef, gentle waters wash coral fragments on to Mandu Mandu Beach. The park's coastline reaches for 50 km

Limestone walls screen Yardie Creek's mangrove-lined estuary

Cape Range National Park

From a high spine of limestone running almost to the Navy communications base at North West Cape, seasonal creeks cut deep gullies to Exmouth Gulf and the Indian Ocean. A park of 50 000 ha occupies the ridge, its seaward slopes and a narrow coastal plain. Though annual rainfall is meagre, cyclonic storms may flood the gullies in summer. Some winter rains can also be expected. But for most of the time the area is parched. Tourists and campers have to plan ahead because the only assured water supply is a bore near the Mangrove Creek, about 5 km inside the northern boundary. Both Mangrove and Yardie Creeks are excellent areas for bird watching.

Cross-country walking is not advised but there are a number of marked trails and walks in the park, of varying grades of difficulty. Some include hides from which to observe the park's bird and animal life. Off the coast of Cape Range is the extensive Ningaloo Marine Park, which protects marine habitats and wildlife, although fishing is allowed at many spots.

Termites take over on heathlands towards North West Cape

Sturt's desert rose, a wild cotton, flourishes in rocky creek gullies, but acacia and eucalypt scrubs predominate

Broken rock litters the shelved walls and floor of Red Gorge, leading west to its junction with three other creek-cut chasms just as deep

Clumps of triodia 'spinifex' deck the heights of Dales Gorge (above and right). Bands of harder rock cross its bed, creating falls and rapids when the creek runs high after the summer wet season, and trapping the cool permanent waters of Circular Pool

Karijini National Park

Plunging chasms break the northern scarp of the sun-baked Hamersley Range, creating surprising oases in an arid plateau of spiky hummock grass and mulga. Scree slopes and steep walls – up to 100 metres high – of conglomerates and shales are darkened by deep bands of rich iron ore and seams of blue asbestos. They shade cool, tree-lined creekbeds.

Of 20 major gorges, most of those accessible to visitors have permanent pools. Dales Gorge, a favourite with campers, is noted for its Fortescue Falls and Circular Pool. Yampire and Kalamina Gorges are also popular. But the sight not to be missed in this huge park of more than 600 000 ha is the crossroads of chasms where Red Gorge is joined by Weano, Hancock and Joffre Gorges. There are walking trails into Red Gorge from Weano and Dales campsites; easy trails from all four camping grounds lead into nearby gorges. Energetic walkers can ascend Mt Bruce by a path that takes about 2 hours.

Karijini National Park

Seen from north of the park, near Wittenoom, the range rises in flat-bedded layers. They are composed of sediments deposited up to 2000 million years ago

Winter sunshine beats into Weano Gorge. Night temperatures may fall below freezing point

Termite mounds are the most obvious signs of animal life above the gorges. Birds are common but most marsupials and reptiles hide in the daytime

Fed by meagre summer rains, the Fortescue River dries up quickly. But an aquifer of ground water runs beside it, supplying the permanent pools at Millstream through springs. Below: Beyond the Fortescue floodplain is country much more characteristic of the arid Pilbara. The Chichester Range rises in the background

MILLSTREAM-CHICHESTER NATIONAL PARK

Four deep, spring-fed pools in the bed of the Fortescue River, descending in succession like a staircase, make a setting that travellers through the hot and dusty Pilbara find difficult to leave. Forests of river red gum and a tropical paperbark called cajeput reach across mudflats of the river's seasonal floodplain. Here and there are tall fan palms *Livistona alfredii*, a species found only at Millstream and in two localities nearby. Warblers and tree-creepers flock to the trees.

Northeast of Millstream, stony hills rise towards the Chichester Range. It is harsh country, sparsely wooded above a ground cover of hummock grasses. But the range itself, heavily eroded by ephemeral creeks, has some cool, densely vegetated gorges. From Snake Creek – one of two camping sites – a 20-minute walk to Python Pool offers a good sampling of gorge scenery. The park, formed by the enlargement of Millstream's boundaries to join up with the former Chichester Range National Park, has a total area of 200 000 ha. It is no place to roam from established routes without ranger advice.

PARKS OF THE CARNARVON & PORT HEDLAND REGIONS

1. Cape Range National Park
400 km N of Carnarvon. Pilbara weather district. Car access off Learmonth–Exmouth road or 40 km past Exmouth.
DESCRIPTION: Page 99.
NOTES: Fee charged for camping and entrance. Take chemical toilet, gas cooker. Fires prohibited. Gas barbecues are located at various sites along the coast.
WARNING: Terrain rugged, waterless. Temperatures often higher in gorges. Beware of heat exhaustion and do not take long walks without informing ranger.
VISITOR CENTRE: At Milyering.
BEST TIME: April to September.
TEL: (08) 9949 1676.
ADDRESS: PO Box 201, Exmouth 6707.

Scenic enjoyment ✓
Day activities ✓✓
Family camping ✓
Hard bushwalking ✗

2. Collier Range National Park
600 km S of Port Hedland. Gascoyne weather district. Great Northern Highway crosses E end of park; dirt access road.
High, deeply eroded ridges and domes dominate a park of nearly 280 000 ha between the headwaters of the Gascoyne and Ashburton Rivers. Spinifex hummock grasses grow sparsely on sandplains and dunes, with mulga, mulla-mulla and some tussock grasses on better soils and eucalypts along creekbeds.
WARNING: Arid, remote area. Travellers far into park must be equipped for outback survival.
BEST TIME: Spring, autumn.
TEL: (08) 9143 1488.
FAX: (08) 9144 1118.
ADDRESS: Box 835, Karratha 6714.

Scenic enjoyment ✓
Day activities ✗
Family camping ✗
Hard bushwalking ✓

3. François Péron National Park
340 km S by road from Carnarvon, about 100 km as the crow flies. Central West weather district. Turn-off North West Coastal Highway at Overlander Roadhouse onto Denham road. Access from Monkey Mia road, 4 km from Denham. Beyond Péron homestead 4WD is essential.
Until recently, the Péron Peninsula was a sheep and cattle station. It was purchased by the state government in 1990 because of the area's outstanding conservation values, and some 40 000 ha of it was established as a national park. It is made up of undulating sandy plains interspersed by gypsum claypans known as birridas. Where the sea has access to the claypans, as has occurred at Little Lagoon and in a more spectacular way at Big Lagoon, shallow inland bays of great beauty are created.
Blue-flowered plants, species such as Dampiera, wild tomato bushes and halganias, abound in the area and, along with white myrtle, yellow wattles and purple peas, form a colourful display in spring. From the cliffs at Cape Péron visitors may glimpse out at sea bottlenose dolphins, dugongs, green and loggerhead turtles.
WARNING: Birridas are unsafe to drive on; bogging will occur. The cliff area at Cape Péron is unstable and must be approached with caution. Bring your own water.
BEST TIME: April to October.
TEL: (08) 9948 1208.
FAX: (08) 9948 1024.
ADDRESS: 67 Knight Terrace, Denham 6537.

Scenic enjoyment ✓✓
Day activities ✓
Family camping ✗
Hard bushwalking ✓

4. Karijini National Park
(formerly Hamersley Range NP) 270 km S of Port Hedland. (450 km by North West Coastal Highway, 550 km by Great Northern Highway.) Pilbara weather district. Car access S from Wittenoom and off Newman road 24 km E of Wittenoom.
DESCRIPTION: Page 101.
NOTE: Basic camping in designated areas. Fees apply.
WARNING: Arid, remote area. Ranger must be notified of walks except for some gorges and at Mt Bruce.
BEST TIME: Late autumn to early spring.
TEL: (08) 9143 1488.
FAX: (08) 9144 1118.
ADDRESS: As for Collier Range.

Scenic enjoyment ✓✓✓
Day activities ✓✓
Family camping ✓
Hard bushwalking ✓

5. Millstream-Chichester National Park
250 km SW of Port Hedland. Pilbara weather district. Wittenoom road from North West Coast Highway crosses park.
DESCRIPTION: Page 104.
NOTES: No drinking water at Chichester Range camps. No camping at Millstream. Fees apply at other sites.
BEST TIME: April to October.
TEL: (08) 9184 5144.
FAX: (08) 9184 5146.
ADDRESS: As for Collier Range.

Scenic enjoyment ✓✓✓
Day activities ✓
Family camping ✓
Hard bushwalking ✓

6. Mount Augustus National Park
430 km from Carnarvon. Gascoyne weather district. Access via Gascoyne Junction, then road that follows Lyons River.
The vast bulk of Mt Augustus is twice the size of Ayers Rock, but as it is clad in low scrub it does not look so spectacular. It is 1105 m above sea level and 1650 million years old. It constantly changes colour from bright red at sunrise through shades of green, blue then through orange and gold at sunset.
The return walk to the summit of Mt Augustus takes 6 hours, but there are several other walks, including a scenic one on the rock's northern side, just off Lyons road, which goes a third of the way up. Aboriginal rock paintings and carvings are signposted.
Over 100 bird species at nearby Edithanna Pool were recorded in in this 9170 ha park in just two days. The vegetation is tall, open mulga shrubland. Several rare plants are known to grow only on the mountains in the area, including a hibiscus, a mulla-mulla and a spectacular native foxglove.
WARNING: Carry plenty of water when climbing to the summit; do not attempt the climb in summer.
BEST TIME: April to October.
TEL: (08) 9948 1208.
FAX: (08) 9948 1024.
ADDRESS: As for François Péron.

Scenic enjoyment ✓✓✓
Day activities ✓
Family camping ✓
Hard bushwalking ✓

7. Rudall River National Park
450 km SE of Port Hedland. Interior weather district. **4WD ACCESS ONLY.**
Dry sand dunes and ridges, salt lakes and the courses of ephemeral streams are protected for scientific study in a park of 1 570 000 ha – Australia's biggest. Scientists used to be the only visitors, so there are no facilities and campers must be self-sufficient.
TEL: (08) 9143 1488.
ADDRESS: As for Collier Range.

① Cape Range NP
② Collier Range NP
③ François Péron NP
④ Karijini NP
⑤ Millstream-Chichester NP
⑥ Mount Augustus NP
⑦ Rudall River NP

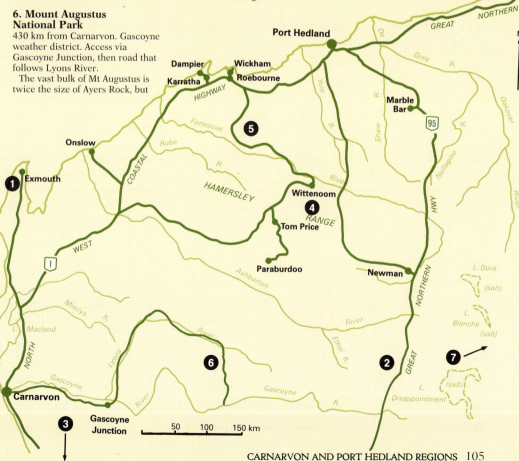

Derby & Kununurra Regions

Lonely no longer, the Kimberleys beckon

DISAPPOINTMENT dogged every pioneering effort to open up the Kimberleys. Gold prospectors and land-hungry settlers first probed the fringes of this immense, broken plateau in 1880. Almost a century later, it remained isolated and forbidding. Its Aboriginal population, as always, was sparse and seasonal. No other high-rainfall district had felt so little human impact.

The Kimberleys have the world's most dangerous calm-weather coast. Tides range as much as 12 metres. Racing in and out of cliffed inlets, they set up eddying currents that boil round craggy islands and over coral reefs.

Inland the plateau is not imposingly high – few peaks exceed 700 metres. But among its abrupt ridges and gullies, 600-1000 km beyond the Tropic of Capricorn, the climate is tyrannical. Hot sunshine beats down for most of the year. From December to March monsoon storms deluge the heights and send violent rivers surging through the gorges. Soils not washed away to the fertile floodplains are shallow and stony. Leached of most plant nutrients, they are valueless except where mineral deposits – including diamonds – have accumulated.

Cattle stations were founded in the 1880s on grassy floodplains skirting the Kimberley block. Beset by stock diseases and dry-season fires, they lent a tenuous existence to Derby and Wyndham, which served them as beef ports. After World War II the decline of both towns seemed irreversible.

Salvation – of Wyndham at least – was promised in the hugely expensive Ord River irrigation project. Initially crops were ruined by disease or raids from the exploding bird population – an unforeseen result of damming the Ord. Today the area has large banana and mango plantations and successfully grows out-of-season crops for city consumption. Lake Argyle and a smaller diversionary lake at Kununurra became fine waterfowl habitats.

Kununurra, built in the middle of nowhere to house irrigation farmers, discovered another reason for being. Modern facilities made it an ideal resting place on the route between Darwin and Derby. While Wyndham steamed beside mudflats and swamps, Kununurra boasted clear boating waters among agreeable bushland. Its recreational appeal gave fresh impetus to regional tourist promotion.

Building roads to link communities in this area of big distances and tough conditions has been an expensive undertaking, with major engineering problems. The last link in the Perth-Darwin route was completed in 1986 with the sealing of the Great Northern Highway between Fitzroy Crossing and Halls Creek. The Gibb River road, a route preferred because of its magnificent scenery, now joins Derby to Wyndham. But nature may still make life hazardous for motorists in these parts: floodwaters swept a road train from the Great Northern Highway north of Halls Creek. Visitors should always check local road conditions.

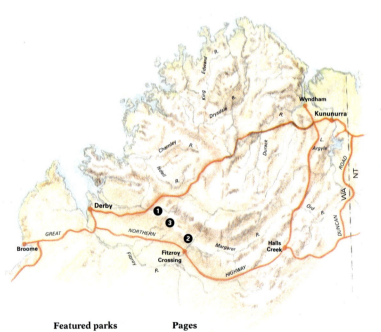

Featured parks — **Pages**
1. Windjana Gorge 108-109
2. Geikie Gorge 110-113
3. Tunnel Creek 114

Your access and facilities guide to all national parks in these regions is on page 115

Geikie Gorge cuts through a fossilised coral reef – built when primeval seas lapped the Kimberleys

Figs and eucalypts crowd Windjana's pools, but sandbanks give walkers some access

Windjana Gorge National Park

Kapok bush flower

Jagged walls of limestone – the fossilised coral of a reef that flanked an invading sea perhaps 300 million years ago – frame a narrow canyon where the Lennard River cuts through the Napier Range. The river flows only in the 'Wet', when the 2100 ha park is inaccessible. But cool, deep pools remain in the shade of the walls, which rise as high as 90 metres. Mixed woodlands of river red gums, other eucalypts and many tropical fig species flourish on sandbanks and spread up into crannies of the heavily weathered rock. Caves above shelter examples of Aboriginal art. Beyond the gorge the woodlands soon give way to a savannah of tussock grasses sparsely dotted with eucalypts, bauhinia and an occasional baobab. Harmless freshwater crocodiles are frequently seen in the gorge, living off the fish that abound in its pools. Colourful birds include jabiru, great bowerbirds, three cockatoo species and many herons. Walks are easy in the gorge area and one pool is usually suitable for swimming. The road passes a ruined pioneer homestead where Pigeon, an Aboriginal Ned Kelly, killed a policeman in 1894.

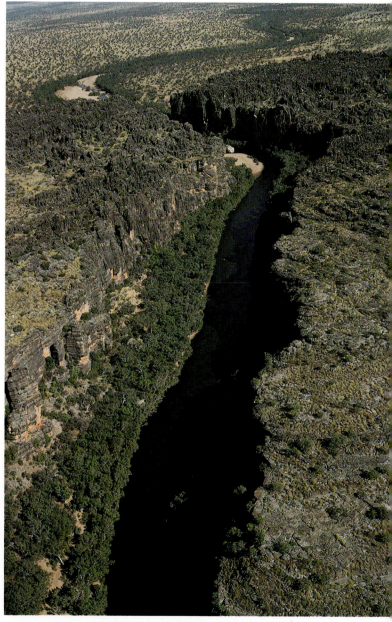

Beyond the gorge, which extends for 4 km through the Napier Range, the Lennard River's dry bed winds across a semi-arid plain. But its grasses are edible tussocks – not spiky 'spinifex'

Left: Vertical grooves in the canyon walls result from trickles of rainwater containing carbonic acid, which dissolves limestone

GEIKIE GORGE NATIONAL PARK

Visitors to the tranquil dry-season pool just south of Geikie Gorge can tell at a glance how they would fare here in the summertime 'Wet'. When the Fitzroy River is flowing, it pushes such a volume of water through the narrow canyon that the weathered limestone walls are bleached to heights of more than 16 metres. The effect of permanent water is seen also on the vegetation, which

Mangroves fringe the gorge walls, which show deep weathering (far left) down vertical cracks

Streamlined for its diving role, a darter rests from fishing. Over 100 bird species seen in the park include kingfishers, herons, great bowerbirds, warblers, parrots and even two kinds of sea eagles

bears muddy watermarks up to 8 metres from the base. But this is not the only striking aspect of nature: the Fitzroy has sawfish and stingray — sea creatures 350 km from any ocean. Their ancestors, like the corals that built the Napier and the Oscar Ranges, were inhabitants of seas that reached around the Kimberley and extended into Central Australia some 300 million years ago. They adapted to a slow transition from salt to fresh water. Also present in big numbers are archer fish, which have mastered the art of shooting down flying insects with jets of water.

The most common kangaroo is the agile wallaby, usually identifiable by a pale stripe on the flank. The Euro and rock wallaby are sometimes sighted. There are many other mammals but they are mostly small, nocturnal and unobtrusive.

Riverbanks in the 3136 ha park are a declared fauna and flora sanctuary. Visitors are not allowed to set foot within 200 metres of the water on either side. A short walking trail loops up to the gorge wall, near boat boarding and launching points. One- to 1½-hour boat tours take in 8 km of the gorge.

Geikie Gorge National Park

The freshwater crocodile is small, and aggressive only when the female is nesting. This one basks below the mud nests of fairy martins

Annual floodwaters of the Fitzroy River wash the lower gorge walls creamy white, below the stains of decomposed plant matter. The dividing line rises as the canyon narrows, showing how the flow is compressed and forced up. Rainfall in the Fitzroy's catchments is seldom more than 500 mm a year – but they cover an area over half the size of Victoria. The flood peak discharge from Geikie Gorge (pronounced 'Geeky' with a hard 'g') is 29 000 cubic metres a second

Chinks in the limestone near the tunnel entrance throw light on to a pool of spring water

Tunnel Creek National Park

The coolest walk in the Kimberleys is not to everyone's taste. Tunnel Creek cuts an underground path for 750 metres through the limestone of the Oscar Range. It is spacious enough – 15 metres wide and never less than 3 metres high. But its clammy darkness can give rise to claustrophobic panic, made more disturbing if the thousands of bats that live here in some seasons are aroused into twittering flight. Walking parties need a powerful torch. They see stalactites descending from the roof in many places, and they may be able to spot Aboriginal paintings. Springs make a permanent flow of water – increased dangerously if the creek itself starts to run.

Halfway along the tunnel the roof has collapsed, allowing bats access to their dark roosting places. At least five species frequent the 90 ha park, including ghost bats and flying foxes (fruit bats)

PARKS OF THE DERBY & KUNUNURRA REGIONS

FACILITIES

 Cabins
 Caravan park
 Equipped picnic area
 Bush camping allowed
Lavatory building

Note: Popular parks without campsites usually have public camping grounds nearby. If in doubt, call enquiries number.

Established campsite
Campsite but no car access

PARK RATINGS: No interest ✗ Some interest ✓ Major interest ✓✓ Outstanding ✓✓✓

1. Purnululu National Park
175 km S of Kununurra. Kimberley weather district. Access off Great Northern Highway 250 km S of Kununurra and 109 km N of Halls Creek on the Spring Creek track. Vehicle access 4WD only. Best viewed from the air; flights from within the park, or from Kununurra, Warmum and Halls Creek. The park is open from April to December, weather permitting.

Purnululu, gazetted as Bungle Bungle National Park in 1987, is a spectacular wilderness of 208 723 ha. It has extraordinary rock formations, a wealth of wildlife and strong links with Aboriginal culture.
NOTE: Facilities are minimal but a ranger station operates seasonally ((08) 9168 7300). Before visiting by road contact the Kununurra office. When in the park advise the ranger of your movements: keep to main tracks.
BEST TIME: May to September.
TEL: (08) 9168 0200.
FAX: (08) 9168 2179.
ADDRESS: As for Windjana Gorge.

Scenic enjoyment ✓✓✓
Day activities ✗
Family camping ✗
Hard bushwalking ✓✓✓

2. Drysdale River National Park
350 km NW of Kununurra. Kimberley weather district. Vehicular access is extremely limited: it is possible to reach the campsite. Visits can also be made by canoe and by helicopter.

Little was known about this remote park of 448 964 ha until a major expedition in 1975. Scientists collected 600 plant species and noted scores of mammals, freshwater fish, birds, reptiles and insects. Low eucalypt forests and woodlands dominate the vegetation with patches of vine thicket around swamps and along watercourses.
BEST TIME: Winter. The park is inaccessible during the Wet.
TEL AND FAX: As for Purnululu.
ADDRESS: As for Windjana Gorge.

3. Geikie Gorge National Park
280 km E of Derby, 20 km N of Fitzroy Crossing. Kimberley weather district. Car access off Great Northern Highway from Fitzroy Crossing. A scenic boat trip, run by the CALM rangers and the traditional aboriginal owners, is a feature of the park. No camping is allowed in the park; good facilities for campers and other accommodation available at Fitzroy Crossing.
DESCRIPTION: Page 110.
BEST TIME: Winter, spring.
TEL: (08) 9191 5121.
FAX: (08) 9191 5165.
ADDRESS: c/o PO, Fitzroy Crossing 6765.

Scenic enjoyment ✓✓✓
Day activities ✓✓
Family camping ✓✓
Hard bushwalking ✗

4. Mirima National Park
(formerly Hidden Valley NP)
3 km E of Kununurra, Kimberley weather district. Car access from town centre.

The road to Mirima from Kununurra's outskirts passes between steep escarpment walls to the 'Hidden Valley'. A nature walk provides information about the plants and animals of the park. Walkers follow a network of interlocking valleys cutting the park's 2068 ha of hilly country. Hummock grasses and scattered baobabs and eucalypts cover stony slopes.
BEST TIME: Winter, spring.
TEL: (08) 9168 0200.
ADDRESS AND FAX: As for Windjana Gorge.

Scenic enjoyment ✓✓
Day activities ✓
Family camping ✗
Hard bushwalking ✓

WARNING
Outback travellers MUST be self-sufficient in all aspects of their trip. Their transceivers should preferably have Royal Flying Doctor Service radio frequencies.

5. Tunnel Creek National Park
180 km E of Derby, Kimberley weather district. Car access off Gibb River road 125 km E of Derby.
DESCRIPTION: Page 114.
BEST TIME: Winter.
TEL: (08) 9191 5121.
FAX: (08) 9191 5165.
ADDRESS: As for Geikie.

Scenic enjoyment ✓
Day activities ✓
Family camping ✗
Hard bushwalking ✗

6. Windjana Gorge National Park
145 km E of Derby. Kimberley weather district. Car access off Gibb River road 125 km E of Derby.
DESCRIPTION: Page 108.
BEST TIME: May to September.
TEL: (08) 9192 1036.
FAX: (08) 9193 5027.
ADDRESS: Box 942, Kununurra 6743.

Scenic enjoyment ✓✓✓
Day activities ✓✓
Family camping ✓
Hard bushwalking ✗

7. Wolfe Creek Crater National Park
510 km S of Kununurra, 150 km S of Halls Creek. Kimberley weather district. Car access off Great Northern Highway 16 km SW of Halls Creek.

A huge iron meteorite, exploding with tremendous power, dug deep into the earth's surface to create a crater 850 m wide. Arid conditions in the flat desert country of the 1460 ha park have kept erosion at a low level. The crater rim, 50 m high, retains its gently sloping symmetry, though windblown sand has filled much of the inner dip. The crater is named after a meandering watercourse to the east.
NOTE: No water supplies in park.
BEST TIME: Winter.
TEL: (08) 9168 0200.
ADDRESS AND FAX: As for Windjana Gorge.

Scenic enjoyment ✓✓
Day activities ✗
Family camping ✓
Hard bushwalking ✗

1. Purnululu NP
2. Drysdale River NP
3. Geikie NP
4. Mirima NP
5. Tunnel Creek NP
6. Windjana Gorge NP
7. Wolfe Creek Crater NP

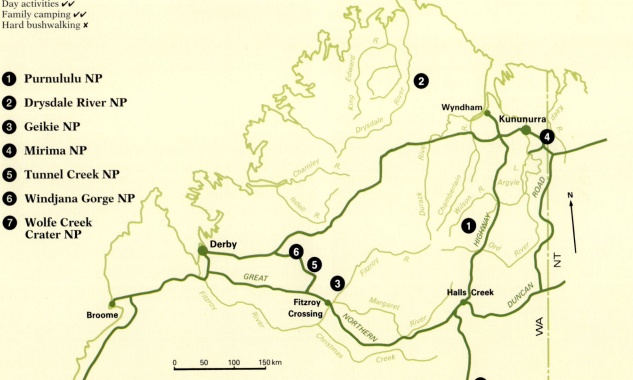

Flowers as food

Because of its big variety of nectar-rich native flowering shrubs and trees Western Australia provides a regular banquet, as well as a home, for honeyeaters. The birds feast on the nectar and pollen of banksia, dryandra, grevillea, hakea, kangaroo paw, emu bush, and flowering eucalypts and paperbarks. But not all honeyeaters are of the feathered variety; there is also the honey-possum, unique to the southwest. In some ways this tiny creature seems to mirror some of the nectar-eating birds: it too has a long brush-tipped tongue and, in place of a beak, a narrow, long, pointed snout which it buries in the flower. It then rapidly flicks its tongue in and out to get the pollen – just like the birds.

Banksia grandis
Honey-possum on banksia

Banksia ashbyi

Kangaroo paw

New Holland honeyeater samples bottlebrush

Bloodwood flower   Grevillea below

Honeyeaters feed on the flowers of the mighty karri while one race of red-tailed black cockatoo lives in karri forest crown and eats eucalypt seeds

Visitor activities in the national parks of Western Australia

Bird watching
   Coastal parks, Geikie Gorge, Stokes, Yalgorup.

Bushwalking
   All national parks but particularly Cape Le Grand, Hidden Valley, Porongurup, Stirling Range.

Camping
   Cape Le Grand, Cape Range, Hamersley, Walpole-Nornalup.

Wild camping
   Bungle Bungle, Walpole-Nornalup (Nuyts Wilderness).

Canoeing/boating
   D'Entrecasteaux, *Kalbarri, Walpole-Nornalup, Walyunga.

Car touring
   Hamersley Range, Nambung, Stirling Range, Walpole-Nornalup.

Caving
   Leeuwin-Naturaliste, Tunnel Creek.

Cave tours
   Leeuwin-Naturaliste, Yanchep.

Cycling
   John Forrest, Leeuwin-Naturaliste, Torndirrup, Yanchep.

Fishing, ocean
   Cape Le Grand, Cape Range (Ningaloo), D'Entrecasteaux, Leeuwin-Naturaliste, Nambung, Stokes, Torndirrup.

Fishing, freshwater
   Geikie Gorge, Millstream-Chichester, Pemberton (Warren River).

Geological studies
   Cape Arid, Fitzgerald River, Geikie Gorge, Hamersley, Leeuwin-Naturaliste, Millstream-Chichester, Nambung, Stirling Range, Windjana Gorge, Wolfe Creek, Yalgorup.

Horse riding
   John Forrest.

Photography
   Bungle Bungle, Fitzgerald River, Geikie Gorge, Hamersley, Hidden Valley, Kalbarri, Leeuwin-Naturaliste, Nambung, Stirling Range, Torndirrup.

Picnicking
   John Forrest, Porongurup, Serpentine, Walyunga, Yanchep.

Power boating
   Cape Range (Ningaloo), Scott River, Walpole-Nornalup.

Orienteering
   Avon Valley, John Forrest, Walyunga.

Rafting
   Avon Valley, *Kalbarri, Walyunga.

A chandelier of stalactites is one of the sights of Yanchep caves

There is the opportunity to photograph wildlife in most parks

Wind blows a fine spume off the waves as a solitary fisherman waits for the telling twitch at his line

Rock climbing
  Porongurup, Stirling Range, West Cape Howe.

Scuba diving/snorkelling
  Leeuwin-Naturaliste, William Bay.

Surfing
  Leeuwin-Naturaliste.

Swimming
  Cape Le Grand, Cape Range, Leeuwin-Naturaliste, Millstream-Chichester, William Bay.

Walking along coastal tracks and beaches
  Cape Arid, Cape Le Grand, Cape Range, Leeuwin-Naturaliste.

Wildflower studies
  Alexander Morrison, Badgingarra, Cape Le Grand, Fitzgerald River, Kalbarri, Stirling Range.

Windsurfing
  D'Entrecasteaux, Leeuwin-Naturaliste, Walpole-Nornalup.

Wildlife observation
  Cape Range, Geikie Gorge, Yanchep.

*The Murchison River flows infrequently and is dangerous in full flood. Permission must be obtained from ranger beforehand.

Wild camping in the new Bungle Bungle National Park

Surfing off Leeuwin-Naturaliste National Park

Signs like these mean business. They are NOT tourist souvenirs as some irresponsible people seem to think. Always heed warnings and take special care in crocodile country.

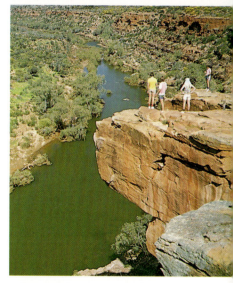

Hikers reach a vantage point overlooking the Murchison River in Kalbarri National Park

---

CAMPING
Wild camping — away from it all, no facilities other than those you create.
Camping — a pit toilet and a tap but no other facilities.
Family camping — established camping ground with showers, toilets, barbecue areas and where you can probably take a caravan, but check beforehand.

DARWIN REGION
Midsummer magic in the monsoon wetlands

BULLDUST – clay in particles as fine as talcum powder – billows with every movement on river flats east of Darwin. It is springtime, and no useful rains have fallen since March. But out over the Timor Sea the clouds are building. By November, heat and soaring humidity enforce a lethargy on most forms of life. Birds reduce their activity. Ants are busy, though – moving to higher ground. The Big Wet is on its way.

Late in the month the first storms break, short but violently intense. Sheets of rain blot out any sight except the flicker of lightning. After New Year, storms brew up every few days. Saturated, the clay plains disappear under water – recalling ancient seas that used to lap the Arnhem Land Escarpment. Lilies, rushes and wild rice spread over the shallows. Waterfowl in hundreds of thousands start a squabbling race for nesting sites. Growth is everywhere in four wet months. On firmer margins trees and vines that were leafless – including even a deciduous eucalypt, the white gum – produce foliage of exaggerated size, quickly followed by flowers and fruit. On wooded savannahs out of reach of the floods the grasses appear. Their nodding seed heads may stand 3 metres high, hiding the huge termite mounds that dominated the winter landscape.

The Wet ends abruptly, and often with vehemence. The autumn return of high-pressure weather patterns may be heralded by southerly gales and rains that flatten the grasses, hastening their death and the desiccation that must follow. By May they are ready as fuel for fires that sweep through most Top End woodlands every winter, sparked by dry electrical storms. Meanwhile the wetlands shrink to billabongs, crowding and barely sustaining fish, amphibians, crocodiles and resident birdlife.

This remorseless regime of monsoon and drought militates against successful settlement of the region. Most attempts to grow crops have failed. The season is too short and diseases are rife. Soils are leached by the perpetual cycle of saturation and evaporation. Even the occupation of Darwin is sometimes threatened: tropical cyclones have wrecked it on four occasions.

Europeans have had an impact on the wetlands, however – and brought them close to ecological disaster. Crocodiles were protected only just in time. Their destruction by hunters would have destroyed the natural balance of food supplies. Even more damaging have been the tramplings of vast herds of water buffalo, descended from imported domestic stock. They crush plant roots and convert clear billabongs into mud.

Under control now in Kakadu National Park, buffalo are at last bringing benefits. The Aboriginal owners derive income from a thriving industry based on what is probably the world's most unusual park facility – an abattoir.

Your access and facilities guide to all national parks in this region is on page 137

Featured parks	Pages
❶ Kakadu	122-129
❷ Katherine Gorge	130-135
❸ Cobourg Peninsula (Gurig)	136

Wetlands of Kakadu – born and reborn in an annual transformation

DARWIN REGION 121

Kakadu National Park

From the Arnhem Land plateau and its forbidding escarpment walls, across the Alligator Rivers flood-plains to the mangrove-choked shores of Van Diemen Gulf, the sweep of Kakadu is immense. Stage 3 was proclaimed in 1988, eight years after the park was established, and the total area of the park is now 1.9 million ha. The biological richness beggars description. Here are well over 900 plant species, nearly 300 kinds of birds, 75 reptiles, 50 native mammals, 30 amphibians, a quarter of all Australian freshwater fish and uncounted thousands of insect species. Kakadu also preserves the most widespread area of early human culture, with evidence of continuous occupation for well over 20 000 years. Its galleries of intricate and varied prehistoric rock art alone would merit the park's World Heritage ranking.

Tourist movements remain concentrated on the upstream reaches of the East Alligator and South Alligator Rivers and on higher country around Nourlangie Rock, with some tourist facilities being developed further south. Pressure is heavy on popular scenic and camping areas in the dry season. Solitude can be found on some long walking trails, but routes must be discussed with rangers and permits obtained.

Acacia in an upland forest

The Arnhem Land Escarpment presents a formidable barrier to the east and south. Seasonal creeks flow from the plateau

Right: Angular faces on Nourlangie Rock are evidence of recent falls

Kakadu National Park

Grassy woodlands of melaleuca and pandanus palm flourish round a billabong west of Nourlangie Rock

Right: Floodplains reach all the way to craggy outliers of the Arnhem Land Escarpment. Most lowlands remain under water for months after the wet season has ended

Below: The wetlands of Yellow Water drain into the South Alligator River near the main tourist facilities at Cooinda

Giant water lilies are sometimes called jacana plants: jacanas (lotus birds) walk over their leaves

Kakadu National Park

Ubirr (Obiri Rock) offers Kakadu's best accessible Aboriginal art – some thousands of years old, some painted this century – with an intriguing variety of styles and subjects. Four sites are easily reached by a 1 km loop track. Two more are passed on a steep climb to a summit lookout

Overhangs of layered, flat-bedded sandstone surround the Ubirr outcrop

The first rock drawings in Ubirr's main gallery can be seen at right. More colourful examples are shown on page 43. Hundreds of similar shelters were used in the wet season by the tribes that hunted in the Kakadu district. Their descendants have been granted ownership of the whole park area, which is leased back to the Canberra-based Australian Nature Conservation Agency

The return of the crocodiles

HUNTED for their valuable skins until the 1960s, the crocodiles of northern Australia were almost wiped out. Under protection they have come back, still increasing in numbers and expanding their range. The freshwater species *Crocodylus johnstoni* is harmless unless a female is defending her nest. This type rarely exceeds 3 metres and is easily distinguished (page 128) by a long, narrow snout. But the short-snouted *Crocodylus porosus*, seen in action here, can grow to 7 metres. It is powerful, increasingly confident against humans, and highly dangerous.

Though capable of ocean cruising and often called the saltwater or estuarine crocodile, it is equally at home in fresh water. It travels up rivers and overland, along chains of billabongs. Some have been seen in the farthest southeastern corner of Kakadu, under the escarpment in the plunge pool of Jim Jim Falls. Throughout the park, more people get close to more crocodiles than anywhere else in Australia. To avoid conflict in certain areas, crocodiles are captured and taken to special farms. But there can be no question of shooting them out again. They are the natural inhabitants of the Kakadu wetlands, and their normal feeding habits are of critical importance to the ecological balance of other species.

Visitors to Kakadu are urged never to swim or paddle in its waterways, nor to fish from riverbanks. Nests and infant crocodiles should never be touched. Anyone coming upon a big crocodile while on foot must avoid getting between the animal and the nearest water.

Crocodiles feed mostly by night, preferring to bask on riverbanks in the daytime

Kakadu National Park

Nitmiluk National Park

More than 100 000 people every dry season take boat tours of the beautiful Katherine River, winding between walls of ancient sandstone that tower up to 100 metres high. Private craft are allowed, except in winter. The canyon, cut here and there by the narrow chasms of tributary creeks, reaches for about 12 km upstream before opening into a wider valley dissecting the southernmost reaches of the Arnhem Land Plateau. Ferns and figs cling to moist crevices in the rock walls; paperbarks and pandanus palms take advantage of sandbanked bends. There is no room to walk up the gorge at water level, but trails leading east from a downstream lookout divert into forested gullies that reach the river at points that offer safe swimming. These routes take 1-4 hours one way. Overnight hikers can continue east for two more days. But the most ambitious of them head north through the 292 000 ha park, along the plateau edge overlooking the valley of Crystal and Seventeen Mile Creeks. Then they traverse westward to the swampy headwaters of the Edith River, coming out after five days at Edith Falls.

Tranquil and depleted in the dry season, the Katherine River has whirlpools and 2-metre waves when summer rains flow in

Wind action in the dry season and torrential downpours in the 'Wet' cause a steady crumbling at the edge of the Arnhem Land Escarpment. Its sandstones and conglomerates, laid down about 1500 million years ago, were compacted and pushed up in a bed of fractured blocks 500 metres deep. Slender palms reaching up from the valley floor are isolated relatives of east coast cabbage-tree palms

NITMILUK NATIONAL PARK

Tropical fig trees crowd a shaded tributary chasm, where conditions resemble those in a rainforest. Soils above are thin and poor

A vertical face of sandstone towers above a little pied cormorant. The park's diverse birdlife includes the rainbow bee-eater, hooded parrot, great bowerbird, bustard and northern rosella. The river has long tom, archer fish and barramundi among many fish species, and freshwater crocodiles are frequently seen

Fallen rock slabs show the wear of summertime flooding

Five-fingered ferns exploit moist soil in overhung crevices

DARWIN REGION 133

Nitmiluk National Park

Vivid pink bark distinguishes salmon gum – more often seen in WA

An assassin bug – a predator of other insects – looks for food on blossoms of calytrix. Heath wildflowers brighten the plateau, but most are seen only after the 'Wet' sets in

Fires are common when the grasses of the plateau's savannah woodlands dry out

Black staining shows the wet-season extent of a tributary waterfall on the Katherine River

Gurig National Park

Cobourg Peninsula reaches west from the coastal margins of Arnhem Land, enclosing Van Diemen Gulf. The whole peninsula and its neighbouring islands, with a total area of 220 000 ha, form a national park under legislation guaranteeing the rights of traditional Aboriginal owners. They collect trophy fees from operators of air-charter 'safaris', bringing in tourists from Darwin to shoot water buffalo – formerly domesticated Indian oxen. Also on the peninsula are wild herds of banteng cattle from Bali, rusa deer from Java and ponies from Timor. All were imported to sustain military garrisons at Raffles Bay (1827-29) and Port Essington (1838-49).

Tropical eucalypt forest dominated by Darwin stringybark and woollybutt covers most of Gurig's flat or gently undulating expanses. But there are also patches of monsoon vineforest, kentia palm thickets, swampy paperbark woodlands and highly developed mangrove forests. Each spring the peninsula is the first southern hemisphere port of call for scores of thousands of migratory birds, and its forests abound with resident species. Dugong and turtles frequent nearshore waters along with many fish species – and big saltwater crocodiles.

Creeks discharge high volumes of water long after the wet season, keeping open gaps in the fringing mangroves and maintaining channels where boats can nose in to sandy beaches

Left: Paperbark forest surrounds clay pans. In summer these are swamps, teeming with native and migrant waterfowl

PARKS OF THE DARWIN REGION

FACILITIES

- Cabins
- Caravan park
- Equipped picnic area
- Bush camping allowed
- Lavatory building
- Established campsite
- Campsite but no car access

Note: Popular parks without campsites usually have public camping grounds nearby. If in doubt, call enquiries number.

PARK RATINGS: No interest ✗ Some interest ✓ Major interest ✓✓ Outstanding ✓✓✓

1. Elsey National Park
310 km S. Katherine weather district. Car access by Stuart Highway, turning off at Mataranka, 110 km S of Katherine. Parts of the park are accessible by gravel roads, which may be closed in the wet season.

The crystal clear headwaters of the Roper River flow in this developing park through outcrops of limestone and sandstone. The salt-laden water deposits its limestone load in the form of encrustations, building up tufa dams across the river. Rainforest pockets and pandanus palms line the banks. The popular Mataranka thermal pool, surrounded by its majestic *Livistona* palms, is included in the park.
BEST TIME: May to September.
TEL: (08) 8975 4560.
ADDRESS AND FAX: As for Nitmiluk.

Scenic enjoyment ✓✓✓
Day activities ✓✓
Family camping ✓
Hard bushwalking ✓

2. Gregory National Park
600 km S, 200 km SW from Katherine on Victoria Highway to Victoria River Crossing or 290 km to Timber Creek. Katherine weather district.

This huge park of about 1.3 million ha protects many Aboriginal and some European heritage sites. Facilities and vehicle access are improving, with a series of 4WD tracks and some 2WD roads. Fishing enthusiasts can reach the river at Big Horse Creek landing, but swimming or allowing children to play near water is not recommended.
VISITOR CENTRE: Timber Creek, Victoria River Crossing, Bullita Homestead.
BEST TIME: May to August.
TEL: (08) 8975 0888.
ADDRESS AND FAX: As for Nitmiluk.

Scenic enjoyment ✓✓✓
Day activities ✓✓
Family camping ✓
Hard bushwalking ✓✓✓

3. Gurig National Park
(Cobourg Peninsula Aboriginal Land and Sanctuary)
200 km NE by air, 550 km by road. Darwin weather district. Restricted 4WD access through Arnhem Land and Murgenella – **COBURG PENINSULA SANCTUARY PERMIT NEEDED.** Road usually impassable December–June. Limited 4WD access within park. Boat access safe only in dry season. Air access from Darwin. **PERMIT NEEDED TO ENTER PARK.**
DESCRIPTION: Page 136.
NOTES: Permit needed for bush camping. Water sources limited – area unsuitable for long-distance walking.
WARNING: Do not swim – area infested with saltwater crocodiles. Box jellyfish may be present November–May.
BEST TIME: May to October.
TEL: (08) 8979 0244.
FAX: (08) 8879 0246.
ADDRESS: PO Box 496, Palmerston 0831.

Scenic enjoyment ✓✓
Day activities ✗
Family camping ✓
Hard bushwalking ✓

4. Kakadu National Park
250 km E (to Jabiru). Darwin weather district. Car access in all weathers by Arnhem Highway to Jabiru. Some internal roads closed in wet season. Check with NT Road Reports (08 8922 3394). Air tours from Darwin, Jabiru.
DESCRIPTION: Page 74.
NOTES: Park fees. Permit needed for bush camping. Billabong water must be boiled before drinking. Bag limits on fishing – no nets or set lines allowed.
WARNINGS: Do not swim – dangerous crocodiles throughout park. Tidal currents and sandbars in East and South Alligator Rivers hazardous to small craft.
VISITOR CENTRE: Jabiru (Bowali), Northern and Southern Entrances.
BEST TIME: May to September.
TEL: (08) 8938 1100.
FAX: (08) 8938 1115.
ADDRESS: Box 71, Jabiru 0886.

Scenic enjoyment ✓✓✓
Day activities ✓✓✓
Family camping ✓✓✓
Hard bushwalking ✓✓

5. Keep River National Park
500 km W, in the Katherine district. Entry 3 km E of NT/WA border on northern side of Victoria Highway.

Victoria River sandstone formations dominate the western side of the park, while the eastern side has impressive bluffs, ridges and gorges, including the Keep River Gorge. Within the 58 000 ha park tropical woodlands meet a semi-arid environment. Enormous boabs punctuate the landscape and luxuriant vegetation fringes pools on seasonal watercourses inhabited by saltwater and freshwater crocodiles.

Weather-worn caves in the sandstone contain Aboriginal engravings and vividly coloured rock paintings. Campfire talks run from June to September (ring for times and dates).
BEST TIME: May to September.
TEL: (08) 9167 8827 or 8973 8770.
FAX: (08) 9168 7396 or 8973 8899.
ADDRESS: As for Nitmiluk.

Scenic enjoyment ✓✓
Day activities ✓
Family camping ✓✓
Hard bushwalking ✓✓

6. Nitmiluk National Park
(formerly Katherine Gorge NP)
330 km S. Katherine weather district. Car access by Stuart Highway and sealed road from Katherine, closed only by major floods. Car access to Edith Falls by sealed road turning off 40 km N of Katherine (may be closed in wet season).
DESCRIPTION: Page 130.
NOTE: Permit required for bush camping. Bush camping not allowed within 8 km of visitor centre.
VISITOR CENTRE: At camping grounds.
BEST TIME: May to September.
TEL: (08) 8972 1886.
FAX: (08) 8971 0702.
ADDRESS: Box 344, Katherine 0851.

Scenic enjoyment ✓✓✓
Day activities ✓✓
Family camping ✓✓
Hard bushwalking ✓✓

WARNING
Outback travellers MUST be self-sufficient in all aspects of their trip. Their transceivers should preferably have Royal Flying Doctor Service radio frequencies.

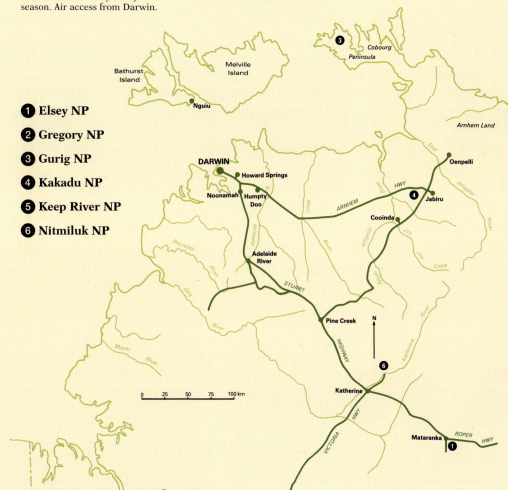

1. Elsey NP
2. Gregory NP
3. Gurig NP
4. Kakadu NP
5. Keep River NP
6. Nitmiluk NP

Spinifex hopping mouse – shelters in a deep burrow system in the heat of the day

Frilled lizard – must open its mouth to raise the frill, the wider the mouth is gaped the more erect the frill

Intermediate egrets – build their stick platform nests in colonies and breed in late summer in the north

Mudskippers – modified fins allow them to hop and skip over tidal mudflats and even climb aerial roots of mangroves

Rainbow bee-eater – before eating its prey beats it on a branch and squeezes it to remove any sting

Black-footed rock-wallaby – a member of the MacDonnell Ranges race, a geographical variant of the species on page 94

Wildlife in the Territory

The Northern Territory divides into two main regions. In the north are wetlands, waterfalls, monsoon forest, mangrove-fringed coastline, pandanus palms, 'magnetic' termite mounds, and waterbirds. In the south are fragile desert environments, ranges and tablelands but with extraordinary reminders – as in Finke Gorge, with its cycads and palm trees – of an earlier, wetter time. It is an area for creatures that over the centuries have become adapted to heat and harsh conditions, that retire to burrows or other shelter when the sun is high and can slow their breathing and heart rate to conserve energy, reduce water loss and help regulate body temperature.

Stripe-faced dunnart – fat stored in the tail is an energy source for when times are hard

Water-holding frog – stores water in sacs beneath the skin before burrowing into the earth to emerge only after the next rains

ALICE SPRINGS REGION

Hidden oases of the rocky Red Centre

RISING abruptly to stark, jagged crests, the parallel ridges of the MacDonnell Ranges make a wall 400 km long across the very heart of Australia. Though it seldom reaches more than 500 metres above the level of the arid plains of red sand, the barrier looks impenetrable – and forbiddingly dry. Hidden in its folds of iron-stained quartzite, however, are courses cut by ancient rivers. It is 20 000 years since any of them flowed year-round. But in their shady chasms are springs and pools, and lush remnants of once-widespread rainforests.

Aranda Aborigines knew all the water sources but used them sparingly. Most pools were left untouched to sustain plants and wildlife. Bans on drinking and swimming were reinforced by a teaching that the conserved pools harboured monstrous watersnakes. To the Aranda the MacDonnells were Altjira – the land that had been there always – and the site of the creation of the first man.

Finding a pass through the MacDonnells became important to Europeans in the 1870s, when an overland telegraph line was laid from Adelaide to Darwin as part of a link between the Australian colonies and Europe. Somehow the wire had to be taken through this hostile region, and a Morse code repeater station must be built there. In 1871 a surveyor found Heavitree Gap – and as a bonus, a bubbling spring in a dry riverbed. He called the river Todd, after his postmaster-general, and the spring Alice, for that dignitary's wife.

Establishment of the telegraph station prompted a surge of further exploration in the ranges, and one by one the many gaps and chasms gave up their secrets. Within a decade they were also giving up their precious waters, and many of their plants, to herds of cattle and sheep that were brought in on pastoral leases.

The retrieval of the Macdonnells' scenic treasures began after World War II when Alice Springs – called Stuart until 1933 – blossomed as a tourist centre. Pastoral leases over the important gap areas were revoked and most by now have been made national parks or nature reserves. But fencing is often needed: in drought the waterholes draw feral cattle and domestic herds from remaining stations, many kilometres away.

In the early days of Central Australian tourism the long side-trip from 'the Alice' to Uluru and Kata Tjuta was a hair-raising adventure that in itself became the high point of many a holiday. Now travellers speed, by air or over a reliable road, to the assured luxuries of an up-to-the-minute tourist village. There are no more surprises – except at the first sight of the great island mountains. In their awesome grandeur, Uluru and Kata Tjuta are still not to be missed.

Your access and facilities guide to all national parks in this region is on page 161

Featured parks	Pages	Featured parks	Pages
❶ Uluru-Kata Tjuta	142-147	❺ Trephina Gorge	154-155
❷ Finke Gorge	148-151	❻ Devil's Marbles	156-157
❸ Ormiston Gorge & Pound	152	❼ Emily & Jessie Gaps	158-159
❹ Simpson's Gap	153	❽ Watarrka	160

A ghost gum survives the harsh conditions of the eastern MacDonnell Ranges

Uluru's grooves and holes result from erosion by a considerable rainfall, averaging about 200 mm but nearer 1000 mm in some years. The run-off near the base supports woodland growth with 'desert oak' casuarinas prominent. Uluru is nearly 9 km in circumference at ground level.

Uluru–Kata Tjuta National Park

Uluru is the local Aboriginal name for Ayers Rock, which is part of a large bed of sedimentary rock. The Rock rises 348 metres above the surrounding plain and changes colour according to variations in light intensity and angle. There is a defined route to the summit, a distance of 1.6 km from the base. The average time for a return trip is two hours. The climb is potentially dangerous and should be attempted only by fit people. Climbing of Mt Olga, the highest of a cluster of 36 domes located 42 km west of Uluru, is not permitted. This formation is also known as Kata Tjuta (many heads).

In 1985 the Uluru/Kata Tjuta Land Trust accepted the title to the roughly 126 000 ha park on behalf of the traditional Aboriginal owners. It was leased to the Australian National Parks and Wildlife Service, and since then has been jointly managed with the traditional owners. Historical points, as well as the park's geology, flora and fauna, are explained on guided tours and in leaflets.

Right: Windblown sands and seeds, caught in hollows, permit some growth of desert grasses and shrubs near the summit of some of the rocks at Katatjuta

Furrowed depressions on a flank of the Rock are called Ngoru – ritual chest scars – by the Aborigines of the area. They occur because some layers of sandstone are tilted so sharply out of the ground that their ends present almost horizontal faces to the weather

Uluru-Kata Tjuta National Park

Perspectives of Uluru
Deceptive distances of the inland: Yulara Tourist Resort is 19 km from Uluru.

An aerial view shows the weathering pattern and Uluru set in its landscape

Glowing at sunrise and sunset, on a stormy day the Rock is dark and mysterious, even more a place of ancestral significance

Uluru–Kata Tjuta National Park

Ghost gum, gaining run-off moisture at the base of Kata Tjuta, is one of very few eucalypts found away from rivers in the Northern Territory. Below: Morning light strikes the entrance to the Valley of the Winds, among the Kata Tjuta cluster.

Tilted strata lines, as well as the vertical grooves of water erosion, can be seen on the Kata Tjuta formations. They are not made of sandstone, in the fashion of Uluru, but of boulder conglomerate. Both were deposited 500-600 million years ago, and thrust up by earth movements some 200 or 300 million years later.

'Old Man' forms the northern prominence of Initiation Rock, where youths of the Aranda tribe underwent rituals marking their entry to manhood. By agreement with local Aborigines the rock may be climbed, but not defaced or littered

FINKE GORGE NATIONAL PARK

Arresting rock forms, carved in red sandstone by seasonal floodwaters and windblown sands, greet travellers after an arduous journey south from Hermannsburg and up the sandy bed of the Finke River. They have entered Palm Valley, the pride of a 46 000 ha park that otherwise consists of a sandplain wilderness. Not far up from the junction of Palm Creek with the Finke – both usually seen as strings of waterholes and soaks – stands Initiation Rock. Its intriguing features can be examined on a 500 metre walking circuit. Beyond is a striking ridge-ringed basin, the Amphitheatre.

Upstream the valley walls close in, reducing evaporation by winds and strong sunlight. Cycads and about 3000 specimens of a unique palm line the creekbed – relics of an age when the whole region enjoyed a wetter climate. A walking trail reaches for 7 km up the valley, accompanied for most of the way by a vehicle track.

Facing 'Old Woman', at the other end of Initiation Rock, a bowl of ritual significance is carved in sandstone

FINKE GORGE NATIONAL PARK

Palm Valley's Livistona mariae *palms grow nowhere else in the world – though they are related to the cabbage-tree palm common on the east coast. In ancient times when seas invaded Central Australia and the general climate was moister, they were probably widespread.*

Left: Macrozamia cycads grow above Palm Creek, sometimes clinging high on the gorge face. Cycads evolved before the palm family: they bear cones rather than flowers, and individual trees have cones of only one sex

Silver-leaf cassia

Acetosa, an introduced weed run wild

Crumbling rock is colonised

ALICE SPRINGS REGION 151

Ormiston Gorge and Pound

Tilted ridges of quartzite, reflecting a dozen colours from the presence of jasper and other silicate compounds, form the high rim of a basin 10 km across. Ormiston Creek and a tributary wander over the basin floor, seemingly puny and often not flowing at all. But in ancient times their floodwaters had the power to breach the western end of the pound, cutting a short but awesome gorge that is the focus of tourist attention.

Sheer faces of red and yellow rock, broken into blocks, hem the boulder-strewn creekbed and a waterhole that is usually suitable for swimming, though not for drinking. There are formed walking tracks at Ormiston. A walk through the gorge – 2.5 km – can be extended into the pound by following the creek upstream. The pound and gorge, along with Simpsons Gap, are both part of the West MacDonnell National Park

River red gums and bloodwoods dot the dry, sandy creekbed, leading out of the pound through a twisting gorge. Euros and wallabies live on the ridges, along with many reptiles

152 ALICE SPRINGS REGION

Evening light strikes broken ridges of the Chewings Range, reflecting (left) in a waterhole beneath

Simpson's Gap

Virtually on the outskirts of Alice Springs, this region of West MacDonnell Park is heavily used by tourists. The eastern wall of Simpsons Gap itself rises 250 metres above the sandy bed of Rose Creek – usually dry. Here and on Cassia Hill, a 500 m walk from the park road, travellers whose time is limited gain a reasonable idea of the nature of the MacDonnell Ranges.

A better representation – with some solitude and a chance to see the park's varied wildlife – is available on the Woodland Walk, leading away to the west from the Cassia Hill carpark. This 8 km walk through scrubland and low hills visits the picturesque Bond Gap. The round trip takes 7 hours. Hardier walkers, equipped with water and overnight camping equipment, can visit other scenic gaps and a number of interesting waterholes.

ALICE SPRINGS REGION 153

Ghost gums (left) and river red gums (below) are thronged year-round by seed-eating birds including the vividly coloured Port Lincoln parrot. Waterfowl come as seasonal migrants

Trephina Gorge

Seasonal tributaries of the Todd River cut two contrasting gorges in a nature park of 1770 ha. Trephina Gorge itself is wide, and sunlight reflecting from its broken red walls – up to 100 metres high – can make it fiercely hot except in the shade of the river red gums growing beside Trephina Creek. John Hayes Rock Hole, formed by another creek in the west of the park, is narrow and shady. Water is held in a deep pool for months after summer rains have passed. Reptiles abound in the rocky environment and many birds of prey hunt overhead. Away from the popular gorges and their picnic areas, quiet vantage points on hills and ridges are easily reached on foot. There are marked walking tracks.

Broken sandstone ledges hold soil for hardy desert plants

Left: Waters of John Hayes Rock Hole, inviting to feral cattle, are often polluted

ALICE SPRINGS REGION 155

DEVIL'S MARBLES

These Eggs of the Rainbow Serpent, as they are called in Aboriginal dreamtime myths, came into being as a single mass formed deep in the earth more than 1500 million years ago. It was cracked into rectangular blocks, then eroded by chemical action as water penetrated all of the joints. Corners took most weathering, so the blocks were slowly rounded. Now the outer layers of the exposed boulders are loosened by daily expansion and contraction. They flake off, leaving cracks in which more chemical erosion starts. In time the Devil's Marbles will be reduced to pebbles

Huge tors of granite, piled high or strewn among hummock grasses, present a startling landmark on an arid and largely featureless plain of quartz gravel. The Marbles – some measuring 6 metres across – are best seen at sunset, when they glow a deep red. Their shade and dew run-off – winter nights are extremely cold – create a micro-climate in which small plants flourish and birds abound. A conservation park covers 1800 ha.

ALICE SPRINGS REGION 157

Emily and Jessie Gaps

Jagged walls of red and white quartzite flank two river-cut openings in the narrowest part of the eastern MacDonnell Ranges, shading near-permanent waterholes. These important gathering places for Aranda Aborigines – Emily Gap has rock paintings on one wall – are also oases for numerous plants and birds. Fairy martins build their side-entry mud nests in rock crannies, and finches and diamond doves flock to river red and ghost gums along the sandy watercourses. Easy walks can be taken from picnic areas at both gaps, and swimming is possible if the creeks are running. The two sites are protected in a nature park of nearly 700 ha.

Desert daisies struggle in a pocket of soil

Early morning sun strikes the west wall of Jessie Gap. The creek's flow is brief but a pool remains for nearly all the year

Plants seize their opportunity around the waterhole at Emily Gap – named, like Jessie Gap, after a surveyor's wife

Left: Sheer quartzite faces, rising behind a ghost gum, were cut in a wetter age when a powerful river found a weak layer in uptilted rock strata

ALICE SPRINGS REGION 159

WATARRKA NATIONAL PARK

Ancient rivers have carved deep gashes, still sharp-edged, in a curiously domed plateau of the George Gill Range. A park of 76 000 ha, formerly called Kings Canyon National Park, has as its focus a maze of gorges occupied by the seasonal watercourses of Kings Creek and its tributaries. These were not fully explored by Europeans until 1960. Rock pools and sandy soaks hold water for all or most of the year, supporting a luxuriant growth of palms, cycads, figs, ferns and cypress pine, attended by prolific birdlife. There is a formed track up to Kings Canyon and its 'Lost City' of domes, some of them pitted with caves. Aborigines sheltered in them until early this century, leaving examples of their rock art. From there on, markers are posted along the trail. Visitors may also take a much shorter walk along the floor of the canyon.

Domes studding the plateau surrounding King's Canyon are shaped by differential erosion of a sandstone block that remained horizontal when it was pushed up. Rivers in an age of much higher rainfall dissected its surface, allowing subsequent weathering – by windblown sand more than water – to work down through layers that are progressively harder

PARKS OF THE ALICE SPRINGS REGION

1. Devil's Marbles Conservation Reserve
390 km N. Barkly weather district. Stuart Highway crosses reserve.
DESCRIPTION: Page 157.
NOTE: Bring own water.
BEST TIME: Autumn to spring.
TEL: (08) 8962 4599.
FAX: (08) 8962 4567.
ADDRESS: Parks & Wildlife Commission NT, PO Box 394, Tennant Creek 0861.

Scenic enjoyment ✓✓✓
Day activities ✓
Family camping ✓
Hard bushwalking ✗

2. Emily and Jessie Gaps Nature Park
12 km E. Alice Springs weather district. Car access via Ross Highway. Check road conditions on (08) 8922 3232.
DESCRIPTION: Page 159.
BEST TIME: Autumn to spring.
TEL: (08) 8950 8211.
TEL: (08) 8951 8268.
ADDRESS: PWCNT, PO Box 1046, Alice Springs 0871.

Scenic enjoyment ✓✓
Day activities ✓✓✓
Family camping ✗
Walking, climbing ✓

3. Finke Gorge National Park
140 km W. Alice Springs weather district. 4WD from Hermannsburg. Last section access road can flood—check conditions on (08) 8922 3232. Coach tours most days.
DESCRIPTION: Page 148.
NOTE: Carry water and all supplies.
BEST TIME: Autumn to spring.
TEL: (08) 8950 8211.
ADDRESS AND FAX: As for Devil's Marbles.

Scenic enjoyment ✓✓✓
Day activities ✓✓
Family camping ✓✓
Walking, climbing ✓✓

4. Ormiston Gorge and Pound (West MacDonnell NP)
130 km W. Alice Springs weather district. Car access via Larapinta and Namatjira Drives. Approach road can flood—check conditions on (08) 8922 3232. Coach tours available.
DESCRIPTION: Page 152.
NOTE: Carry drinking water.
BEST TIME: Autumn to spring.
TEL: (08) 8950 8211.
ADDRESS AND FAX: As for Devil's Marbles.

Scenic enjoyment ✓✓
Day activities ✓✓
Family camping ✓✓
Walking, climbing ✓✓

FACILITIES

 Cabins
 Caravan park
 Equipped picnic area
 Bush camping allowed
 Lavatory building
Established campsite
Campsite but no car access

Note: Popular parks without campsites usually have public camping grounds nearby. If in doubt, call enquiries number.

PARK RATINGS: No interest ✗ Some interest ✓ Major interest ✓✓ Outstanding ✓✓✓

5. Simpsons Gap (West MacDonnell NP)
23 km W. Alice Springs weather district. Car access off Larapinta Drive. Coach tours daily.
DESCRIPTION: Page 153.
NOTE: Total fire ban—gas cooking only. Entrance fee. No pets.
BEST TIME: Autumn to spring.
TEL: (08) 8952 3131.
ADDRESS AND FAX: As for Devil's Marbles.

Scenic enjoyment ✓✓✓
Day activities ✓✓
Family camping ✗
Walking, climbing ✓✓

6. Trephina Gorge Nature Park
75 km E. Alice Springs weather district. Car access off Ross Highway.
DESCRIPTION: Page 155.
NOTE: Water available at some campsites.
BEST TIME: Autumn to spring.
TEL: (08) 8950 8211.
ADDRESS AND FAX: As for Devil's Marbles.

Scenic enjoyment ✓✓
Day activities ✓✓
Family camping ✓
Walking, climbing ✓

7. Uluru-Kata Tjuta National Park
450 km SW. Alice Springs weather district. Car access W from Stuart Highway on Lasseter Highway. Entrance fee. Buses, airline flights daily to Yulara Tourist Resort.
DESCRIPTION: Page 144.
NOTE: Camping and accommodation in Yulara Tourist Resort, outside park.
WARNING: Uluru climbers should be realistic about their fitness. Wear rubber-soled shoes and keep to marked track.
VISITOR CENTRE: Near Uluru.
BEST TIME: Autumn to spring.
TEL: (08) 8956 3138.
FAX: (08) 8956 3139.
ADDRESS: ANPWS, PO Box 119, Yulara 0872.

Scenic enjoyment ✓✓✓
Day activities ✓
Family camping ✗
Walking ✓✓

8. Watarrka National Park
(formerly Kings Canyon NP)
310 km SW. Alice Springs weather district. Car access via Mereenie Loop and West MacDonnell NP or Luritja Road from Yulara and the Lasseter Highway.
DESCRIPTION: Page 160.
BEST TIME: Autumn to spring.
TEL: (08) 8950 8211.
ADDRESS AND FAX: As for Devil's Marbles.

Scenic enjoyment ✓✓✓
Day activities ✓✓
Family camping ✓✓
Walking, climbing ✓✓

① Devil's Marbles Conservation Reserve
② Emily and Jessie Gaps Nature Park
③ Finke Gorge NP
④ Ormiston Gorge and Pound (West MacDonnell NP)
⑤ Simpsons Gap (West MacDonnell NP)
⑥ Trephina Gorge Nature Park
⑦ Uluru-Kata Tjuta NP
⑧ Watarrka NP

Bearded dragon – mouth agape, beard erect, ready to frighten off its enemies

Desert death adder – during the day is usually part-buried in sand and difficult to detect; also unwilling to move, so beware

Juvenile perentie – full-grown specimens average 1.6 metres but can reach 2.5 metres in length

Reptiles of the inland

Although not 'cold-blooded', most reptiles have low body temperatures. Their warmth must come largely from outside sources; they cannot cope with extreme conditions. After the chill of the night, they are lethargic until warmed by the sun, and as they warm so their colours become lighter. The desired temperature established, they then alternately bask and shelter to maintain it. Such inefficient circulation systems mean that few reptiles can sustain any rapid activity for long.

Thorny devil, Moloch horridus – neither horrid nor devilish, just a tiny slow moving anteater

Central netted dragon – stays on open ground even in high temperatures when others shelter

Centralian blue-tongued lizard – lives among spinifex in sandy desert and has taken on the colouring of the landscape

In Keep River, tribal area of the Miriwung people, a number of caverns are decorated with engravings and paintings

Tourist boats cruise the course of the Katherine River where it has sliced through the Arnhem Plateau. But those who set out to explore Nitmiluk National Park on foot, get a much more real appreciation of its variety of plants and its rugged scenery.

CAMPING
Bush camping — away from it all, no facilities other than those you create.
Camping — a pit toilet and a tap but no other facilities.
Family camping — established camping ground with showers, toilets, barbecue areas and where you can probably take a caravan, but check beforehand.

Visitor activities in the national parks of the Northern Territory

Aboriginal culture
Emily and Jessie Gaps; Gregory; Kakadu; Keep River; Nitmiluk; Uluru.

Abseiling
Gregory.

Aerial tours
Kakadu; Nitmiluk.

Bird watching
Elsey; Emily and Jessie Gaps; Finke Gorge; Gregory; Gurig; Kakadu; Keep River; Nitmiluk; Ormiston Gorge and Pound; Simpsons Gap; Trephina Gorge; Watarrka.

Boat tours
Kakadu; Nitmiluk.

Bush camping
Finke Gorge; Gregory; Kakadu (permit needed outside certain designated sites); Nitmiluk; Ormiston Gorge and Pound; Watarrka.

Bushwalking
Devil's Marbles; Elsey; Emily and Jessie Gaps; Finke Gorge; Gregory; Kakadu; Keep River; Nitmiluk; Ormiston Gorge and Pound; Simpsons Gap; Trephina Gorge; Watarrka.

Camping
Devil's Marbles; Elsey; Gregory; Gurig; Finke Gorge; Kakadu; Keep River; Nitmiluk; Ormiston Gorge and Pound; Trephina Gorge.

Canoeing/boating
Elsey; Gregory; Kakadu; Nitmiluk.

Car touring
Gregory; Kakadu.

Cycling
Kakadu.

Family camping
Elsey; Kakadu; Nitmiluk.

Fishing, freshwater
Elsey; Gregory; Kakadu; Nitmiluk.

4-W driving
Gregory.

Geological studies
Elsey; Finke Gorge; Gregory; Kakadu; Keep River; Nitmiluk; Ormiston Gorge and Pound; Simpsons Gap; Trephina Gorge.

164

A tour group prepares to set up camp at the Devil's Marbles

National parks provide an ideal outdoor classroom

4WD vehicles have made many of the more remote and difficult areas accessible to outback enthusiasts

Historical studies
Gregory; Kakadu.

Horse riding
Gregory; Kakadu.

Liloing
Nitmiluk.

Orienteering
Nitmiluk.

Power boating
Gurig; Kakadu.

Rafting
Nitmiluk.

Rock climbing
Gregory; Keep River; Watarrka.

Scuba diving/snorkelling
Nitmiluk.

Surviving skills/journey testing
Kakadu.

Swimming
Elsey; Emily and Jessie Gaps; Finke Gorge; Nitmiluk; Ormiston Gorge and Pound; Watarrka.

Walking along coastal tracks and beaches
Gurig.

Wildflower studies
Elsey; Emily and Jessie Gaps; Finke Gorge; Gregory; Gurig; Kakadu; Keep River; Nitmiluk; Ormiston Gorge and Pound; Simpsons Gap; Trephina Gorge; Watarrka.

Wildlife observation
Devil's Marbles; Elsey; Emily and Jesse Gaps; Finke Gorge; Gregory; Gurig; Kakadu; Keep River; Nitmiluk; Ormiston Gorge and Pound; Simpsons Gap; Trephina Gorge; Watarrka.

NOTE: Photographing Aboriginal sacred sites is not permitted, nor should visitors photograph Aboriginal people.

Crocodile country
Signs like these mean business. They are NOT tourist souvenirs as some irresponsible people seem to think. Always heed croc warnings, even when there are no visible signs of their presence. In crocodile territory you can't afford to be careless: get local or expert advice before swimming, camping, fishing or boating.

The waterhole in Ormiston Gorge and Pound brings welcome relief from the heat

INDEX

A

Aboriginal sites 43, 75, 108, 114, 122, 127, 140, 148-9, 158, 160
Acacias 21, 24-7, 81, 122
Acetosa hop 151
Alexander Morrison 91
Alice Springs 12, 140
Alligator Rivers 122
Ants. harvester 27
Aranda tribe 140, 148, 158
Archer fish 111
Arnhem Land 10, 26, 140
  Escarpment 122, 125, 131
Artesian water 16
Assassin bug 134
Atmospheric pressure 12
Ayers Rock 10, 142, 144-5
Avon Valley 91

B

Badgingarra 91
Banksias 24, 27, 59, 64
Banteng cattle 136
Baobab 21
Barren Ranges 56
Basalt 10, 15
Bat, ghost 39
Bats 114
Beach formation 18-19
Beech 22-23
Beedelup (see Pemberton)
Beedelup Falls 80
Bell-fruited mallee 59
Belinup Hill 66
Bibbulmun Track 70
Biosphere reserve 59
Bites and stings 34
Black Point 83
Bluff Knoll 52
Bogong High Plains, Vic. 40
Boorabbin 68
Bremer Bay 56
Brigalow 25
Broke Inlet 83
Brooks, John 96
Buffalo, water 41, 120, 136
Bushfire 34-5

C

Calothamnus (see One-sided bottlebrush)
Calytrix 134
Camels 27
Cape Arid 46, 66-7, 68
Cape Le Grand 46, 60-1, 68
Cape Leeuwin 46
Cape Range 96, 98-9, 105
Cape Vancouver 62
Cape York Peninsula, Qld. 12, 14, 23
Carnarvon 96
Cassia, silver-leaf 151
Cassia Hill 153
Casuarinas 24, 27, 142
Cats, feral 41
Cave formations 78-9
Cervantes 84
Chewings Range 153
Chichester Range 104

Christmas Island 105
Cinnamon fungus 25, 70, 166
Clematis 77, 81
Climate 10, 12, 16, 20-1
Coasts and islands 18-19
Cobourg Peninsula Aboriginal Land and Sanctuary (Gurig NP) 136, 137
Collier Range 105
Coneflower 55
Conifers 20
Continental drift 20
Coral 10, 18, 43, 107
Cormorant, little pied 133
Cotton, wild 99
Cottonhead 75
Cradle Mountain-Lake St Clair 23, 34, 42
Crocodiles 35, 112, 128-9
Crystal Creek 130
Curry flower 64
Cyanophytes 20
Cycads 20, 21, 151

D

D'Entrecasteaux 70, 82-3, 91
Daisies 26, 158
Dales Gorge 97, 101
Damage to parks 31, 32, 36, 40-1
Dampier, William 96
Darling Scarp 11, 70, 72, 75, 90
Darter 111
Darwin 120
Deep River 48, 49, 50
Deer 31, 136
Derby 106
Desert daisy 158
Desert oak 142
Dieback 25, 70
Diplolaena 87
Distress signals 34
Downy stackhousia 61
Drovers cave 92
Dryandra 55
Drysdale River 115

E

East Alligator River 122
East Mt Barren 56
Eastern Highlands 11, 14-15, 16, 18, 20
Edith Falls 130
Enamel orchid 60
Epacrids 27
Ephemeral plants 26
Epiphytes 22-3
Epping Forest 38
Erosion 10-11, 14-15, 18-19
Esperance 46
Esperance Bay 60
Eucalypts 21, 24-25, 51, 70
Eucla 68
Eungella 23, 39
Evaporation 12
Everlastings 26
Evolution of plants 20-1, 24-5
Exmouth 96, 99
Exmouth Gulf 99

F

Feral animal damage 40-1
Fern, five-fingered
Figs 20, 23
Finke Gorge 140, 148-51, 161

Fire 12, 21, 24-5, 34-5
Fitzgerald Beach 57
Fitzgerald River 38, 46, 56-9, 68
Fitzroy Caves 39
Fitzroy Crossing 106
Fitzroy River 110, 113
Five-fingered fern 133
Flinders Bay 83
Forests 20-5
Fortescue Falls 101
Fortescue River 104
Frankland River 48, 51
Franklin River, Tas. 42
Frank Hann 69
Fraser Island, Qld 18, 43
Frenchman Peak 61
Fresh water 16-17
Frog, gastric-brooding 38, 39
Frost 12-13
Funnel-web spider 34

G

Gardner Lake 94
Geikie Gorge 106, 107, 110-13, 115
Geology 14-15
George Gill Range 160
Ghost bat 39
Ghost gum 141, 146, 155, 159
Gibb River 106
Glacial action 14, 15
Gloucester NP (see Pemberton)
Goat, feral 41
Golden-shouldered parrot 39
Gondwanaland 10-11, 20, 22-3
Goongarrie 69
Gooseberry Hill 92
Granite 10-11
Grass-trees 27, 47, 55, 90
Grasshopper, Leichhardt's 38
Grasslands 21, 26
Great Barrier Reef 42, 43
Greenmount 92
Gregory 137
Grevillea 27, 87
Guinea flowers 87
Gums, ghost 141, 146, 155, 159
  river red 55
  salmon 134
  snappy 26
Gurig 120, 136, 137

H

Hairy-nosed wombat 38
Hakea 58
Halls Creek 106
Hamelin Pool 20
Hamersley Inlet 56
Hardenbergia 77, 81
Hassel 69
Hassel Beach 62
Hastings River mouse 38, 39
Heat waves 12
Heathlands 27
Heaths 27, 54
Heavitree Gap 140
Hell Fire Bay 60
Heritage Commission, Aust. 17, 43
Hibiscus 57
Hopetonn 56
Houtman Abrolhos Islands 18
Hovea 55
Hummock grasses 26, 101

I

Igneous rocks 10
Indian Ocean 77
Initiation Rock 148-9
Iron Range 39
Islands 19

J

Jacana plant 125
Jane Brook 72
Jarrah 25, 70, 81
Jim Jim Falls 128
John Forrest 70, 72-3, 92
John Hayes Rock Hole 154

K

Kakadu 16, 33, 38, 42, 43, 120, 121, 122-129, 137
Kalamunda 70, 90, 92
Kapok bush flower 108
Kalbarri 16, 70, 71, 86-9, 92
Karijini 10, 15, 26, 96, 97, 100-2, 105
Karri 50, 81
Kata Tjuta 10, 142, 143, 146, 147
Katherine River 130, 133, 135
Keep River 137
Kimberleys 10, 12, 15, 16-17, 25, 106
King George Sound 46
King's Creek 160
Kingia grass-tree 55
Kununurra 106

L

Lake Argyle 16, 22, 106
Lakes 16, 17
Lambertia 58
Lamb's poison 82
Landforms 10-11
Le Grand Beach 60
Leeches 35
Leeuwin-Naturaliste 70, 76-9, 92
Leichhardt's grasshopper 38
Lennard River 108, 109
Leschenaultia 64
Lesmurdie Falls 92
Lignotubers 24, 26
Limestone 10
  caves 78-9
Little pied cormorant 133
Livistona mariae palm 150
Long Point 48
Long Pool 75

M

MacDonnell Ranges 10, 15, 140, 141, 153, 159
Malee 26, 27, 59
Maleefowl 38, 39
Mandu Mandu Beach 98
Mangroves 18
Margaret River 77
Marri 25, 81
Marron 80
Metamorphic rock 10
Mid Mount Barren 56
Millstream-Chichester 96, 104, 105

Millstream palm 21
Mirima 115
Mitchell grass 26
Moates Lake 62
Moisture 12-13, 16-17
Monsoon 12, 23, 120
Moore River 92
Mosses 20
Mount Arid 66
Mount Bruce 101
Mount Conner 10
Mount Giles 152
Mount Le Grand 60
Mount Manypeaks 47, 62
Mount Olga 142
Mount Ragged 66
Mountain bell 54
Mountain pea 55
Mountains 10-15
Mouse, Hastings River 38, 39
Mulga 26
Mungo 12, 16
Murchison Gorge 71, 86
Murchison River 86, 87
Murray River 16, 25
Myrtle beech 22

N

Nambung 70, 84-5, 92
Nambung River 84
Nandewar Range, NSW 14
Napier Range 108, 111
National park management 30-33, 35
Negrohead beech 22, 23
Neerabup 92
Nitmiluk 120, 130-5, 137
Noisy scrub bird 62
Normans Beach 62
Nornalup Inlet 46.48, 49
North Stradbroke Island, Qld 40
North West Cape 12, 96, 99
Nourlangie Rock 123
Nullarbor 27
Numbat 38
Nuyts, Pieter 46, 48
Nuyts Wilderness 48

O

Oak, desert 142
Obiri Rock (see Ubirr)
Oil drilling 96
Olgas (see Kata Tjuta)
One-sided bottlebrush 72
Open forests 24-5
Orchids 23, 27, 60, 61
Ord River 16, 106
Ormiston Creek 152
Ormiston Gorge and Pound 140, 152, 161
Oscar Range 111, 114
Oxylobium 63

P, Q

Palm Creek 148, 151
Palm Valley 148, 150
Palms
 distribution 20, 23
 Livistona mariae 150
 Millstream 21
 pandanus 124
Paper heath 54
Paperbarks 25, 27, 72, 83, 136

Park worker 33
Parrot, golden-shouldered 39
Peak Charles 69
Peas 55, 64, 82
Pelsaert, Francis 89
Pemberton 70, 80-1, 92
Perth 11, 70
Pets in parks 37
Phyllodes 26
Piesse Brook 90
Pigeon (Aboriginal outlaw) 108
Pigs, feral 41
Pilbara 104
Pimelea 90
Pines
 distribution 20
 pencil 20
Pinnacles Desert 84, 85
Planning a visit 37
Plant evolution 20-1, 24-25
Poached-egg daisy 26
Point Ann 56
Point d'Entrecnsteaux 82, 83
Point Gardner 62
Porcupine grass (see Hummock grasses)
Port Hedland 12, 96
Porongurup 69
Possum, striped 39
Powers of rangers 33
Prickly bitter pea 64
Prince Regent River 17
Psyllids 25
Public participation 36
Purnululu 8-9, 115
Purpose of national parks 30-1
Python Pool 104
Quarry Bay 76
Quokka 65

R

Rainfall 12-13
Rainforests 22-3
Rangers 32-33
Recherche Archipelago 60, 66, 67
Red Gorge 100
Redback spider 34
Regeneration 24-5
Restoration of parks 40-1
Rhyolite 10, 15
River redgum 25, 155
Rivers and lakes 16, 17
Rock art 43, 108, 114, 122, 127, 158, 160
Rock types 10, 14-15
Roe Creek 153
Rossiter Bay 60
Rongh Range 99
Royal hakea 58
Rudall River 30, 105
Rufous tree-creeper 80
Russell Range 66

S

Society and survival 34-5
Salmon gum 134
Salt production 96
Saltbush 26, 27
Sand
 mining 40
 movement 18-19
 types 18
Savannah 134
Sawfish 111
Scaevola 84
Scarlet banksia 64

Scott 93
Scrublands 26, 27
Sedimentary rocks 10
Serpentine 93
Seventeen Mile Creek 130
Shale 10
Shannon Forest Park 93
Shark Bay 20
Shores 18-19
Shothole Canyon 96
Signalling for help 34
Silver tea-tree 61
Silver-leaf cassia 151
Simpson's Gap 140, 153, 161
Slate 10
Smokebush 54
Snake Creek 104
Snakebite 34
Snowy River 36
Soil types 15, 26-27
South Alligator River 122
Southern cross 64
Southern Ocean 46, 48, 56, 60, 83
Southern plains banksia 59
Spider bites 34
Spider orchid 61
Stackhousia, downy 61
Stingray 111
Stings and bites 34
Stirling Range 46, 52-5, 69
Stirling Range smokebush 54
Stokes 69
Striped possum 39
Sturt's desert rose 99
Sugarloaf Rock 76
Sunshine 12
Survival and safety 34-5
Swan River 28, 75

T

Tan wattle 81
Tasmanian tiger 39
Tathra 93
Tea-trees 58, 61
Temperature 12, 14
Termite mounds 99, 103
Thistle Cove 60
Thomas River 66
Thylacine (Tasmanian tiger) 39
Tick bites 34
Tides 18-19, 106
Timor Sea 120
Tingle 51
Todd River 140, 155
Toolbrunup Peak 53
Torndirrnp 69
Trachyte 10, 15
Trade winds 12
Tree evolution 20-1, 24-5
Tree ferns 25
Tree-creeper, rufous 80
Trindia (see Hummock grasses)
Tunnel Creek 106, 114, 115
Turtle 33
Tussock grasses 26-7, 109

U, V

Ubirr 43, 126-7
Uluru-Kata Tjuta 15, 140, 142-7, 161
Valley of the Winds 146
Van Diemen Gulf 122, 136
Vegetation 20-7
Volcanoes 10-11, 14-15
Voluntary park work 36

W

Walpole 48
Walpole-Nornalup 24, 46, 48-51, 69
Walyunga 28-9, 70, 74-5, 93
Walyunga Pool 75
Wandoo 25, 73
Warren River 80
Watarrka 10, 140, 160, 161
Water buffalo 41, 120, 136
Water lily 125
Watheroo 93
Warsonia 90
Wave action 18-19
Waychinicup River 62
Weano Gorge 102
Weather patterns 12, 13
West Cape Howe 69
Wetlands 17, 120
White spider orchid 61
Wilderness Society 36
Wildlife conservation 38-9
Willandra Lakes. NSW 16, 26, 42-3
William Bay 69
Wilsons Promontory, Vic. 22, 23, 36
Windjana Gorge 106, 108-9, 115
Winds 14
Wolfe Creek Crater 115
Wombat, hairy-nosed 38
Woodlands 21, 24-5
Woofoleo Brook 75
World Heritage List 42-3
Wyndham 106

Y

Yakka (see Grass-trees)
Yalgorup 93
Yalgoup Cave 78-9
Yanchep 93
Yardie Creek 89
Yellow Water 125
Yokinup Bay 66

OTHER FEATURED PARKS

Devil's Marbles Conservation Reserve 10, 140, 156-7, 161
Emily and Jessie Gaps Nature Park 140, 158-9, 161
Mount Manypeaks Nature Reserve 46, 62-5, 69
Trephina Gorge Nature Park 140, 154-5, 161
Two Peoples Bay Nature Reserve 46, 62-5, 69

Protect our parks and wildlife

- Observe all fire bans.
- Use only fireplaces provided, or your own portable cooker.
- Don't take cats or dogs with you.
- Don't take firearms or other hunting weapons.
- Don't leave litter.
- Don't disturb or remove plants, rocks or animals.
- Obey 'No Entry' signs - they are for your safety, and also protect fragile areas.
- Keep your vehicle to formed roads and marked parking areas.

Addresses

Park Services

Environment Australia Biodiversity Group
GPO Box 636, Canberra ACT 2601 (02)6250 0200
Environment ACT
PO Box 144, Lyneham, ACT 2602, (02)6207 9777
New South Wales National Parks and Wildlife Service
PO Box 1967, Hurstville, NSW 2220, (02)9585 6444
Department of Environment
PO Box 155, Brisbane Albert Street, Qld, 4002, (07)3227 7111
Queensland National Parks and Wildlife Service
PO Box 155, Brisbane Albert Street, Qld, 4002, (07)3227 8186
Great Barrier Reef Marine Park Authority
PO Box 1379, Townsville, Qld, 4810, (07)4750 0700
South Australian National Parks and Wildlife Service
GPO Box 1047, Adelaide, SA, 5001, (08)8204 9000
Department of Environment and Land Management
Division of Conservation and Land Management
PO Box 44A, Hobart, Tasmania 7001. (03)6233 8011
Parks Victoria
Level 2, 35 Whitehorse Rd, Deepdene, Victoria 3103.
13 19 63
Department of Conservation and Land Management
Locked Bag 104, Bentley Delivery Centre, Western Australia 6983, (08)9334 0333

Park Associations

National Parks Association of the ACT
Maclaurin Crescent, Chifley ACT, 2606 (02)6282 5813
National Parks Association of NSW
PO Box A96, Sydney South, NSW 1235, (02)9223 4660
National Parks Association of Queensland
PO Box 1040, Milton, Queensland, 4064, (07)3367 0878
Nature Conservation Society of South Australia
120 Wakefield St, Adelaide, SA 5000 (08)8223 6301
Tasmanian Conservation Trust
102 Bathurst St, Hobart, Tasmania 7000, (03)6234 3552
Victorian National Parks Association
10 Parliament Place, East Melbourne, Victoria 3002, (03)9650 8296
WA National Parks and Reserves Association
219 Railway Pde, Maylands, WA 6051, (08)9370 5901

Foundations for Conservation

Australian Conservation Foundation
Head Office : 340 Gore Street, Fitzroy, Victoria 3065.
(03)9416 1166
National Parks Foundation of South Australia
100 Currie St, Adelaide, SA 5000. (08)8231 0016
Foundation for National Parks and Wildlife
GPO Box 2666, Sydney, NSW 2001. (02)9337 3388

Australian Trust for Conservation Volunteers

Head Office : 15 Lydiard St, North Ballarat, Vic 3353.
(03)5333 1483
Vic : 534 City Rd, South Melbourne, Vic 3205.
(03)9686 5554
NSW : 2 Holt St, Stanmore, NSW 2048. (02)9654 1244
ACT : Old City Parks Depot, White Crescent, Campbell, ACT. 2602 (02)6247 7770
Qld : Old Government House, George St, Brisbane, Qld 4000. (07)3210 0330
NT: 3 Harvey St, Darwin, NT 0800. (08)8981 9095
WA: 216 Queen Victoria St, North Fremantle, WA 6159. (08)9336 6911
SA: State Tree Centre, Broadway Drive, Campbelltown, SA 5074. (08)8207 8747
Tas: Salamanca Arts Centre, Salamanca Place, Hobart, Tas 7000. (03)6224 4911

Wilderness Society

National Office : 130 Davey St, Hobart, Tas 7000.
(03)6234 9799

Bushwalking Federations

NSW : Bushwalking Federation of NSW, GPO Box 2090, Sydney, NSW 1043, (02)9548 1228
Vic : VicWalk, 241 Swan St, Richmond, Vic 3121, (03)9421 3100
Qld : Queensland Federation of Bushwalking Clubs, GPO Box 1573, Brisbane, Qld 4001
WA: WA Federation of Bushwalking Clubs, PO Box 851, Scarborough, WA 6922, (08)9362 1614
Tas : Federation of Tasmanian Bushwalking Clubs, PO Box 1190, Launceston, Tasmania 7250.

Youth Hostels Association

NSW : 422 Kent St, Sydney, NSW 2000. (02)9261 1111
NT : 69 Mitchell St, Darwin, NT 0800. (08)8981 6344
Qld: 154 Roma St, Brisbane, Qld 4000. (07)3236 1680
SA: 38 Sturt St, Adelaide, SA 5000. (08)8231 5583
Tas: 28 Criterion St, Hobart, Tas 7000. (03)6234 9617
Vic: 205 King St, Melbourne, Vic 3000. (03)9670 7991
WA: 236 William St, Northbridge, WA 6003 (08)9227 5122

Acknowledgments

The publishers and editors are deeply indebted to administrators, interpretation officers and rangers of the various national parks services. Countless people spent long hours supplying or verifying information. Others assisted in planning the touring photographer's itineraries, or gave him considerable help in the field.

Thanks are also due to the staff of the National Herbarium, Royal Botanic Gardens, Sydney, for their assistance in plant identification, and to botanist A. R. Rodd.

Reference sources: The publishers acknowledge their indebtedness for information gained from the following books: *Atlas of Australian Resources* (Division of National Mapping); *Australia, a Timeless Grandeur*, Helen Grasswill (Landsdowne Press); *Australian Vegetation*, R. H. Groves, ed. (Cambridge University Press); *Australia's Endangered Species*, Derrick Ovington (Cassell); *Australia's 100 Years of National Parks* (NSW National Parks and Wildlife Service); *Complete Book of Australian Mammals*, Ronald Strahan, ed. (Angus and Robertson); *Discover Australia's National Parks*, Robert Raymond (Ure Smith); *Discover Australia's National Parks and Naturelands*, Michael and Irene Morcombe (Landsdowne Press); *Life on Earth*, David Attenborough (Reader's Digest-Collins-BBC); *National Parks of New South Wales*, Alan Fairley (Rigby); *National Parks of New South Wales* (Gregory's); *National Parks of Queensland*, Tony Groom (Cassell); *National Parks of Victoria*, Alan Fairley (Rigby); *National Parks of Victoria* (Gregory's); *National Parks of Western Australia*, C. F. H. Jenkins (National Parks Authority of WA); *Regional Landscapes of Australia*, Nancy and Andrew Learmonth (Angus and Robertson); *The Face of Australia*, C. F. Laseron, revised by J. N. Jennings (Angus and Robertson); *The Franklin Blockade*, Robin Tindale and Pam Waud, eds (Wilderness Society); *The Heritage of Australia* (Macmillan, Australian Heritage Commission); *The Value of National Parks* (Australian Conservation Foundation).

Photographs

The cover picture and most other photographs were taken by Robin Morrison, except for: (t = top, c = centre, b = bottom, l = left, r = right) 11: t, Richard Woldendorp; b, Research School of Earth Sciences, ANU. 20: b, Photo Index. 28-9: Richard Woldendorp. 30: b, Dept of Conservation Forests & Lands, Vic. 31: l, cb, Sutherland Shire Library. 32: tl, bl & br, Dept of Conservation Forests & Lands, Vic. 33: tl, Ian Morris, Australian NPWS; br, Queensland NPWS. 34: Tasmanian NPWS. 35: cl, Tasmanian NPWS; tr, Bob Mossel; br, Jeffery Cutting. 36: t, Queensland NPWS; b, Dept of Conservation Forests & Lands, Vic. 37: Conservation Commission of the NT. 38: tl & bl, Hans & Judy Beste; tr, Stephen Donellan; br, R. C. Lewis, CSIRO Division of Entomology. 39: tl, R. & A. Williams, National Photographic Index; tc & tr, Hans & Judy Beste; br, Ralph & Daphne Keller. 40: r, and 41: tl & br, Dept of Conservation Forests & Lands, Vic. 41: bc, Graham Robertson; tr, New South Wales NPWS. 42: t, C. Veitch. 44-5: J. M. La Roque/Auscape. 72-5 and 90: Richard Woldendorp. 94: tl, Cliff Winfield; bl, Esther Beaton/Auscape; tr, br, Jean-Paul Ferrero/Auscape. 95: tl, Jiri Lochman/Auscape; tr, Esther Beaton/Auscape; cl, bl, br, Cliff Winfield. 116: tl, tr, bl, Cliff Winfield; br, Jean-Paul Ferrero/Auscape. 117: tl, cl, bl, Cliff Winfield; tr, James Rule/ANT; br, Graeme Chapman/Auscape. 118: tr, br, WA Dept Conservation & Land Management; bl, Cliff Winfield. 119: tr, cl, WA Dept Conservation & Land Management; bl, Cliff Winfield. 138: tl, tr, Hans & Judy Beste/Auscape; cl, bl, Jean-Paul Ferrero/Auscape; br, Graeme Chapman/Auscape. 139: t, Hans & Judy Beste/Auscape; bl, B. Thomson/National Photographic Index; br, R. Jenkins/National Photographic Index. 144: t, b, Michael Jensen/Auscape. 145: Jean-Paul Ferrero/Auscape. 162: All by Jean-Paul Ferrero/Auscape. 163: tl, Jean-Paul Ferrero/Auscape; tr, M. W. Gillam/Auscape; b, Jiri Lochman/Auscape. 164: tl, Cliff Winfield. 164-5: NT Conservation Commission.

Printed and bound by Dai Nippon Printing Co. Ltd, Hong Kong